KNITLANDIA

A Knitter Sees the World

×××

CLARA PARKES

STC CRAFT / NEW YORK

Published in 2016 by Stewart, Tabori & Chang
An imprint of ABRAMS

Library of Congress Control Number: 2015948556

ISBN: 978-1-61769-190-4

Editor: Melanie Falick
Designer: Sebit Min
Production Manager: True Sims

The text of this book was composed in Archer.

Printed and bound in the United States

10 9 8 7 6 5 4 3 2 1

Stewart, Tabori & Chang books are available at special discounts
when purchased in quantity for premiums and promotions as well as
fundraising or educational use. Special editions can also be created
to specification. For details, contact specialsales@abramsbooks.com
or the address below.

115 West 18th Street
New York, NY 10011
www.abramsbooks.com

PREFACE: In Motion

WHEN I WAS SIX, I went with my mother on a run to the grocery store. Too busy to fiddle with the garage door when we got back, she parked the car in the driveway and went inside, letting me snooze as she often did. Eventually I woke up, unbuckled myself, and came in for lunch. A few minutes later, a man in uniform knocked on our door and said, "Your car is on fire."

A plume of smoke billowed from the frame of what had been, until a few minutes earlier, our trusty VW Bus. A fuel line must've snapped, they said, spilling gasoline onto the still-hot engine until it ignited. All four tires had melted and the windows had shattered into a million tiny pieces. You'd think the experience would have put me off cars completely. Strangely enough, it didn't. If anything, it only reinforced my desire to set the wheels in motion, as if the real danger were in sitting still.

I grew up with grand road trips, coast-to-coast adventures in unreliable cars, playing Mad Libs and counting license plates. After my parents' divorce, my mother moved us to Tucson, where we found smaller ways to escape. Some weekends, after giving up on waiting for a boyfriend to call, she'd mutter a curse and load us into the car. Windows open, we chased the sunset down Speedway Boulevard until the streetlights and sidewalks gave way to empty desert and the tall shadows of saguaros.

We snaked our way up, up, up, until a sudden sharp left turn took us over Gates Pass. Ahead, the view opened up to nothingness. Back down the mountain we went, to an empty desert floor. We'd find a spot and pull over. The moment the car went silent, the desert took over. A brilliant city of lights unfolded in the sky above as our eyes grew accustomed to the darkness. My mother would lie on the hood of the car; my brothers and I, like rattlesnakes, preferred the warmth of blacktop on the empty road. The desert air smelled sweet and exotic. Lying there, my entire area of vision was filled with stars. At any minute, it felt like gravity would reverse and the sky would suck me in. I'd fall up, up, up into the cosmos.

Eventually my mom would call to us and we'd get back in the car. As soon as we drove back through Gates Pass, the lights of Tucson would twinkle in the distance, like jewels on black velvet, beckoning us home. We hadn't gone far, but that brief interlude away, even just over the pass, fulfilled my need to wander.

My first "real" job after college was as a travel writer for a pre-Internet publisher. Rarely did my fellow writers and I go anywhere. We called venues and interviewed people who had no idea they were being interviewed. We scoured sources, worked with stringers on location, and managed to piece together fresh, original information. We became masters of the blurb. Colleague John Pinson and I even won an award from the Society of American Travel Writers Foundation for our work. The year was 1995.

When that job ended and I moved into high-tech publishing, I became a business traveler. From convention center to conference center to major hotel chain I'd go, from lobby to ballroom back to airport, to cover events with names like Database and Client/Server World and DB Expo. I'd sit in product briefings with various VPs of technology, and every second felt like a race to see if I could get out before they realized how little I understood.

I was still working at my day job in high-tech when I launched my online knitting magazine, *Knitter's Review*, in 2000. My goal was to be the eyes and fingers for knitters during a time when our world was exploding with new yarns, tools, books, gadgets, and events. That fall, I ventured to my first sheep-and-wool festival. It was in Vermont, and I called the number listed on the program to ask a question. The woman was quite friendly, and before long, she was offering me her home for the weekend. "I'll be up at the lodge anyway," she said, "so you'd have the place all to yourself."

I declined, figuring she might also be the kind of person who kept dead cats in her freezer. But when I got to the show, that same friendliness prevailed. Nobody knew who I was or what I was up to, they were just being—or at least they seemed to be—genuinely nice. They were eager to share their stories, answer my questions, and offer advice. The interactions energized me. I enjoyed it so much that I went to another festival, then another, then another.

Knitting has offered me a perfect lens through which to see the world. During my fifteen years writing *Knitter's Review*, I've clocked so many miles that I've essentially taken off or landed once every two weeks. My destination has never been a shiny skyscraper or boardroom. I've been headed to a yarn store, a spinning mill, a sheep-and-wool festival, perhaps a hotel or conference center taken over, even if only briefly, by knitters. The specifics of the trips varied, but my underlying mission was always the same. I have become a yarn evangelist, and I travel in search of my congregation.

The stories in this book follow those years, beginning in 2000, when the Internet was in its relative infancy, when email newsletters such as mine were still a novel way to reach and build community among what we thought was a small group of knitters online. They track the rise—and occasional fall—of our important gatherings, our people and places, landmarks and legends, each of which has played a vital role in the vibrant knitting culture and community that exist today.

CHASING A LEGEND IN TAOS

ONCE UPON A TIME in a Taos, New Mexico, grocery store, a woman named Luisa Gelenter was going about her business buying food. Somewhere in the produce section, she felt a person standing too close. Inching away, she kept shopping, only to feel this person creep up on her again. Annoyed, she stomped off to another aisle. When the lurker soon reappeared, Luisa turned and snapped, "What do you want?" The words were barely out of her mouth when she recognized it was Julia Roberts. The movie star and avid knitter happened to be a big fan of Luisa's work and was too shy to introduce herself.

Who knows how it really played out, but that's the story Luisa loved to tell.

In the world of yarn, Luisa Gelenter was a legend. Using nothing more than water and select minerals, bugs, skins, branches, roots, leaves, petals, and powders, from knowledge she picked up in Bolivia in the early 1970s, she could transform natural fibers, such as humdrum wool and mohair, into vibrant, magical yarns for knitting, weaving, and other creative pursuits. Some of her yarns were ultimately spun by a machine at a mill, but in the beginning, all of her fiber was farmed out to a squad of loyal handspinners who produced luminous, lively, color-laden skeins that were truly one of a kind. A complete garment in these yarns cost a fortune and was worthy of any red carpet.

In 1974, Luisa had opened a shop called La Lana Wools, which occupied the old Bert Phillips studio in the center of Taos. As Phillips had helped establish Taos as a hub for artists, so did Luisa for lovers of natural dye. While tapestry weavers flocked to Taos to learn from the legendary Rachel Brown, from the late 1970s until the early part of this century, La Lana was a mecca for anyone interested in natural dyes or fibers colored with them.

Luisa's yarns were outliers at a time when other yarn stores were selling the spun equivalent of Hamburger Helper. Most were made from small batches of naturally dyed fibers that had been blended and spun by hand, aided by a discerning human eye, into unrepeatable skeins. They were priced by the ounce, like gold. Because of the incredible amount of time and skill each one required—and the appropriately high price tag for such work—she owned this market and had no competitors.

I'd come to town for the Taos Wool Festival when I first set eyes on La Lana. October in New Mexico is chile time, and the air was filled with that distinct fragrance of chiles being roasted outdoors. The leaves were beginning to turn in the Sangre de Cristo Mountains, but in town, pink hollyhocks and Russian sage still lingered, striking a lovely contrast against the warm adobe walls.

The festival took place at Kit Carson Park in the center of town. There, a carefully juried group of vendors was assembled in a broad circle, like a wagon train at the end of the day. In the middle, a fiddler and guitarist played tunes while people danced on the grass. The setting was magical.

La Lana wasn't a vendor that year, I suspect for the simple reason that the shop was adjacent to the park. So I dutifully left and crossed the street, walking through a small courtyard and into La Lana.

The minute I entered the store, I was greeted by an army of finished garments. It was like the wardrobe trailer on an exotic film set, with wildly textured vests and tunics that looked like a cross between native tapestries and ceremonial garb. The clothes would overwhelm a shy person. These pieces required grandeur. Rumor was Julia owned at least one.

Beyond the garments, the room opened up into a space I can only describe as a yarn cathedral. It still had the original massive wall of north-facing windows from when it was Phillips's studio. But instead of illuminating paint on canvas, the windows now showcased Luisa's masterpiece on the next wall: a writhing waterfall of handspun skein upon skein of explosive color and texture unlike anything I'd ever seen. Brilliant mohair locks shimmered against matte wool fibers that seemed to be still in the process of twisting together. It was so stunning, so rare and spectacular, that you could only stop and gasp. It was the kind of place that made you talk in a whisper.

I was tongue-tied. All I could do was furtively snap a few pictures, buy some skeins, and sneak out. After I wrote about that visit in *Knitter's Review*, I heard from Luisa and we began a cautious, respectful correspondence.

When I next went to Taos a few years later, it was specifically to see Luisa. I was writing *The Knitter's Book of Yarn* and needed to know more about the mechanics of yarn. Luisa happened to have a mill at her disposal. In 1991, she'd launched the Taos Valley Wool Mill with two partners. One of the partners was a man named Robert Donnelly, an industry veteran Luisa touted as her guru in all things yarn. "He can tell you everything," Luisa said. I needed to know everything, so when a family wedding was announced in New Mexico, I emailed Luisa and we made a date.

I arrived with family in tow, depositing them at our hotel before walking over to La Lana for what I thought would be a short visit. This time, I went up to the woman behind the register, introduced myself, and asked to see Luisa. To calm my butterflies, I pretended to study a basket of dyestuff.

A booming voice came from behind. Everyone seemed to step aside—if not physically, then energetically—to make room for the short, stocky, weather-beaten woman who'd just come in.

I took a deep breath, smiled, and held out my hand. But Luisa didn't take it. "No," she shook her head. "You're not Clara. You're too young."

I didn't know her well enough to tell if she was serious or not, but she looked angry. All my confidence drained, and I suddenly felt like a kid, a poseur. She was probably in her sixties, such a legend that she had assistants and protégées to do grunt work. She'd mistaken me for someone on her level when, in fact, I was just starting out.

We recovered with small talk, and she showed me around the shop. Remembering why I'd come, she asked, "Shall we go see Robert?" The mill was outside of town. We would need to drive there, she explained. Did I have a car? I stuttered that mine was parked at the hotel across from the . . . "Oh forget it," she shook her head, "I'll drive."

This was not the start I'd had in mind.

We got into an ancient Volvo, me carefully moving things off the pas-
senger seat. The car was filthy. Not *Hoarders* filthy but the kind of chaotic
filth you'd imagine in Jackson Pollock's car. Amid the empty plastic tubs
and scratched cassette tapes was a sort of barnyard debris from her foraging expeditions. I imagined her screeching to a halt by the side of the road,
grabbing the bucket, diving into a thicket, and emerging triumphantly
with the very twigs necessary to obtain a rich orange or copper or red.
What looked like desert brush to us was, in fact, her paint box.

We drove slowly out of town, making our way farther and farther until
there was nothing but desert. Just as I began to wonder if I should've brought
an overnight bag, we reached Arroyo Hondo and turned off the road.

Amid the single-wide trailers, barbed-wire fences, abandoned cars,
and barking dogs was a small, nondescript building. Its doors were open,
and an immense noise was coming from within. This was the mill.

The minute we went inside, I was hit by the overwhelming smell of
lanolin mixed with spinning oil. The space itself was quite small, about the
size of my local garage, just big enough for key pieces of equipment.
I remember spotting the bobbins before anything else. Bins of empty ones,
bins of full ones, bobbins tucked on shelves and tossed in cardboard boxes.

A man with a beautiful black ponytail was dropping tidy clumps of
fiber onto a conveyor belt that led into the drum carder, a huge machine with
whirring cylinders. I gasped as a frothy river of fiber poured from the other
side of the machine right onto the concrete floor. A sudden urge came
over me to lie on that floor and let the fibers spill over me—but I resisted.

The spinning frame stood idle, its long row of bobbins empty and
expectant. Nearby, I saw slinky strips of white fiber being pulled into a
noisy green contraption, spewing out the other end like soft-serve ice
cream into a tall cylindrical bucket.

Something wasn't working right. An older man in a gray T-shirt
flipped a switch, lifted the lid, and pulled away some fiber. Another man,
this one with a gray beard and a Miller Racing baseball cap, stood with
him and consulted on that little clump of fiber, both of them pointing,
nodding, rubbing it between their fingertips, shaking their heads. They

must've agreed on something, because the baseball-cap man nudged the fiber back into the machine, closed the lid, and flipped the switch back on. Spotting us, he smiled and came over. This was Robert.

He gave me a cursory tour of the mill. I'd seen the carding machine, which, Luisa explained, was at the heart of her experiments with millspun dyed yarn. The more they could control the fibers as they went in, the more unique the results they could get on the other end when it came time to spin. I didn't quite understand at the time, but I nodded eagerly.

Another spinning frame was in motion, strands of fiber worming their way from tall barrels to bars suspended over the machine, then through a series of rollers until spun yarn wound its way onto bobbins. Nearby, yarn snaked its way upward from cones, over another bar, through more loops, and was then paired with another strand before getting twisted together onto a bigger bobbin as plied yarn.

Robert yelled an explanation over the noise, but to be honest, the sights and sounds and smells were so overwhelming that I barely heard what he was saying. I just knew I was in love with this place.

At last, we ducked through a back door and sat down on white plastic lawn chairs in the dirt. Luisa and Robert sat with their backs to the wall, facing the afternoon sky. I could see large pebbles where the adobe walls had begun to wash away.

Luisa smoked. I held my breath until the breeze changed, then quickly filled my lungs with clean air before the smoke blew back again. I watched the cigarette as it got smaller and smaller, until, *whew*, she stubbed it out. She probably had asked if I minded her smoking, but after our bumpy start, I was certainly not going to tell Luisa Gelenter not to light up.

We sat there talking about yarn—about the current state of the knitting world, about the state of domestic textiles, about the fate of larger mills across the country. Robert had worked at many of them and witnessed their demise firsthand. Now, he operated a fraction of what he was used to, serving a very different audience. Instead of running ten hours a day to satisfy the voracious appetites of T-shirt or towel manufacturers, he was spinning small batches of wool for handweavers, knitters, and hobby farmers, people who cared about the breed integrity of their flock and knew each animal by name. Farms in the region tended to have Navajo-Churro sheep, or alpacas and llamas, even angora goats, animals who generally grew long, strong fiber. Robert set this up as a semi-worsted spinning mill with equipment that had been carefully chosen and calibrated to process these fibers. He also made yarns for Luisa.

When I brought up my passion for breed-specific wool yarn, Robert shook his head. He'd approached several breed associations over the years to try and get them to pool their fibers and spin special yarns from them. But back then, in 2006, nobody was interested yet. It turns out Robert was a man ahead of his time.

Whenever the conversation lagged, Luisa would pull out yet another cigarette. Robert, whose yellowed mustache suggested a lifetime of smoking, preferred to nibble on sunflower seeds, spitting the shells into his hand and dropping them on the ground. Every few minutes he'd pop another one in his mouth, and the two of them would launch into another story—mostly about people I didn't know but they assumed I did. My interview skills were still abysmal, and I was so intent on impressing them, on proving I wasn't that upstart kid Luisa had thought I was, that I didn't dare reveal the depths of my ignorance.

On the subject of making yarn, however, Robert gave answers that have guided me well all these years. He cautioned me about the importance of starting with good fiber. "You can't make good yarn out of bad fiber," he explained, before adding, "but you *can* make bad yarn out of good fiber." Holding the keys to the good and the bad? The people operating your mill equipment. "Oh," he added, "and always get your carding waste back. They'll just try to sell it to someone else."

Eventually, the sun slipped below the horizon and the neighborhood dogs started howling. My family would be worried about me; it was time to go. We said our farewells, leaving a heap of butts by Luisa's chair, a mound of sunflower-seed shells by Robert's, pages of words scribbled in my notebook.

My yarn book came out a year and a half later, and the Maine Morning Mitts pattern—designed using Luisa's yarn and offered as a free

download—became a runaway success. For me, they were a fitting tribute
to the beauty of Luisa's colors, like knitted jewels for the hands. I know she
was pleased and proud, but also a wee bit annoyed that the pattern called
for just one skein.

Luisa and I would email back and forth occasionally. When she
friended me on Facebook, I knew I'd passed the test. She would comment
on my posts, usually something like asking about a rug in the background
of a photo I'd taken. When she forwarded me emails with subject headers
like, "Fwd: Fwd: HOW A DOG HUGS A BABY . . . ABSOLUTELY
PRICELESS," I'd finally become a friend.

As the years passed, the knitting world changed. Carefully nurtured
relationships with magazine editors were no longer enough to stay on top,
nor was having Julia Roberts as a customer. Ravelry arrived and, around
that same time, the rise in so-called indie designers. Instead of being told
what yarn to use by a publisher with advertisers to please, these designers
got to pick whatever they wanted—often the least expensive yarns they
could find or the ones offered to them free. That wasn't Luisa's way. She
was a shrewd businesswoman, and giving away yarn to unproven strangers didn't seem to be in her nature.

Along with the indie designers came indie dyers, filling the market
with fresh new machine-washable wools in electric, acid-dyed colors we
would affectionately refer to later as "clown barf." Nuanced natural hues
had no place under that circus big top. La Lana remained a pilgrimage
stop for traveling knitters, but over time they left with fewer and fewer
skeins in their bags.

They say the hardest thing for a musician is to play quietly, and the
same is even more true for hand-dyers. While she'd built her reputation
upon vividly nuanced skeins, by now Luisa was experimenting with the
most intriguing and extraordinary yarns of her career—which also ended
up being the least known.

Eternally curious and with a mill at her disposal, Luisa had been
exploring the notion of using minimal color to define an otherwise white
space. Whereas before she relied on handspinners to blend the colors, now

she was doing it right at the mill, layering dyed fiber by hand, in varying intensity, atop undyed fiber as it entered the carding machine. She'd hinted at it in my visit, when we'd been looking at the carding machine. Once I had a skein of the yarn in my hands, I understood.

You see, the carding machine is to textiles what sifting is to flour, that essential first step in producing clump-free cohesion. It is built to blend. But Luisa and Robert were figuring out when and how to add color in such a way that it would remain distinct all the way through carding, pin-drafting (that green machine that was giving Robert trouble), and the final spin. It's the most complex and demanding thing you can try, something you can only do if you control the mill equipment yourself—or have a really good working relationship with the person who does. You're hacking a machine whose entire purpose is to mix, tricking it into barely doing its job. On a large scale, Eisaku Noro in Japan is the only other person who's ever managed to do this successfully.

The results were astounding in their silence. Skeins of white puffy singles, upon closer examination, revealed traces of color that were distinguishable down to their individual fibers. As you knit, the color would gain intensity, then fade away again. It looked effortless, and perhaps that was the problem. By then, the expectation was that La Lana would remain a museum for beautifully colored handspun yarns. Here, you had barely any color at all, and it was masterful. But it wasn't enough.

In February 2012, news came that La Lana was closing. It was the end of an era. "Faithful customers who could be counted on to drop a couple hundred dollars in wool and supplies have all but disappeared," Luisa told the *Taos News*. "Plus, I'm getting old. We all are."

A whole new batch of natural dyers had cropped up. Some had taken classes with Luisa, others knew her only vaguely by name. Whereas Luisa had learned her trade in South America, these newcomers had found their passion in places like India and Japan. They had blogs and Ravelry fan pages and Etsy shops.

But for La Lana to close, for Luisa to take down her shingle from lack of business, it was as if Georgia O'Keeffe had gone out for groceries and returned to find that all of the other artists and galleries had abandoned New Mexico, leaving her with nothing but a stack of canvases, some back issues of *Knitter's Magazine*, and a hefty rent payment coming due.

After the announcement, Luisa was inundated with messages and orders for remaining inventory. "We are so sad about our closing," she wrote me. "Well I am sad about it too . . ." She explained that she'd still offer her dyeing services for private clients, and I made a mental note to ask her about collaborating with me on my Great White Bale project. I promised to spread the word about her closing sale and I wished her the best of luck.

Later that July, she sent me a quick email about a yarn I'd just mentioned in *Knitter's Review*. Apparently someone *aquí en Taos* (although born and raised in New York City, Luisa often veered into Spanish when she wrote) was planning on opening a yarn store in Taos with the same name as the yarn. "Will this be a problem for her?"

I was annoyed at being asked something I had no authority to answer, so I never replied.

On December 8, 2012, I learned that Luisa had died.

Melanie Falick, who'd spent time with Luisa while writing *Knitting in America*, later told me Luisa had been diagnosed with cancer. She left behind a son, Aaron, who works as a plumber in Santa Fe.

Upstairs in my barn studio, right next to my first-edition copy of *The Principles of Knitting* and dog-eared Barbara G. Walker books, is my shrine to Luisa. It contains several skeins of her yarn that I've never had the courage to knit. Every time I try to think of a suitable project, Luisa's voice interrupts me. "Oh God, not the mitts again." She shakes her head. "You want to blend me with Cascade 220? Are you *loco*?!"

In death, Luisa Gelenter has become one of those larger-than-life people about whom you tell stories to the young folk around that proverbial campfire. They nod, doing their best to imagine, to try and understand. But they will never quite grasp how exciting and awe-inspiring Luisa's work was. She was the real deal, the kind of person who could leave even a glamorous Hollywood superstar momentarily speechless.

FROM BASEBALL TO BROADWAY: Swatching in the Big Apple

KNITTING CONFERENCES used to have a reputation for taking place in Atlantic City or Oakland or maybe a ski resort in Michigan's Upper Peninsula during the off season. They were rarely in what you'd call "top-tier" destinations. The hotels usually had a free airport shuttle, dreadfully slow elevators, and lobbies that smelled like a swimming pool.

But when *Vogue Knitting* threw its hat into the event ring in 2011 with Vogue Knitting LIVE, it was a point of pride that its first show take place in the city most powerfully associated with the magazine and, in fact, with anything sporting the name *Vogue*: the Big Apple.

We gathered for three days in early January at the Hilton Midtown between West 53rd and West 54th Street, just up from Times Square, one long block from Fifth Avenue and within a Warhollian paint splatter of the Museum of Modern Art.

Every knitter of note had been invited, from Debbie Stoller (Yale-educated editor of *BUST* and author of *Stitch 'n Bitch*) and Meg Swansen (legendary daughter of the equally legendary early media maven Elizabeth Zimmermann) to Stephanie Pearl-McPhee (two-time *New York Times* bestselling author and possibly the only woman alive who can fill a convention center with sock knitters). They were there, along with nearly every author, designer, and teacher I'd ever known or admired—50 teachers in all, and more than 250 classes. It was a three-ring circus of the very best, most awe-inspiring kind.

Instead of gum-chewing staff who spell your name wrong and express awe at how far you've traveled ("Wow, Maine? Really?"), here we had doormen and corridors of elevators and glistening marble floors that looked like they'd just been cleaned with a Zamboni. In the midst of it all was the deeply incongruous but irrefutable presence of knitting. Skeins of yarn had been arranged along the top of the check-in counter. A tall, glitzy event banner hung proudly by the main doors that opened onto Sixth Avenue.

The event was a three-day embodiment of, "If you build it, they will come." More than 2,500 students and 6,000 market-goers converged for the inaugural show. Many traveled from afar, excited to have a reason to venture into New York City. Others emerged from nearby brownstones and co-ops and condos. Like superheroes responding to the Bat Signal of knitting, they came.

Some were regulars, the kind who can rattle off the names of every conference they've attended for the last twenty years. These are the knitting groupies who collect names and experiences.

"To tell you the truth," one might say, "I wasn't that pleased with the accommodations at Stitches East."

Her friend would interrupt, "But they had that buffet. . . ."

"Oh you're right," she'd reply, "that was good. But the parking, that was highway robbery."

They'd both nod and look around the room, arms folded, collecting more observations to discuss back in their hotel room.

For others, this was a first. I had an elegant, fur-clad woman in my yarn class. She wore diamond earrings the size of swimming pools, and she'd never heard the word "handspinner" before—nor did she understand what my explanation, "someone who spins yarn by hand," meant. Yet, she was a knitter, the deeply intuitive kind who was probably taught by her mother (or nanny) at such an early age that it was instinctive now. She knew the *how*, and I was able to teach her the *why*—why, for example, she wanted a silk blend for that fine, flowing pleated skirt she was about to begin.

These events are the closest we have to our own university, to tenured professors and a formal curriculum. Because we lack sufficient financial clout to establish a permanent place for such learning, we have this traveling circus of experts who roam from town to town, event to event, squeaky-wheeled suitcases of samples in tow. Instead of vacuum cleaners or encyclopedias, we sell knowledge and skill acquired from decades of experience.

Our classes covered everything from cables and Estonian lace to welts, reversible color knitting, and, in my case, yarn. Some taught entire classes dedicated to helping you complete one pattern; others focused on technique and theory.

At the heart of it all, we were pitching inspiration. We taught the dream that you *can* make these things at home. And through achieving that dream, and with the ensuing confidence that brings, you feel a few inches taller after conquering something you honestly didn't think you could do. Some run marathons to get this feeling, others knit. Some, like Susie Hewer, run marathons *and* knit and set Guinness World Records for it.

In our cozy bubble, it was easy to forget where we were or that anyone else was staying at the hotel. A brief elevator ride was all it took, a friendly smile, a glance at our name tag, a double-take, an exclamation of, "*Knitting*, huh?" followed by an awkward silence until they reached their floors.

Knitters, like nurses and librarians, seem doomed to stereotype. As Stephanie Pearl-McPhee first pointed out, there are more knitters in North America than golfers. We represent one of the largest consumer population segments. Yet we continue to be pigeonholed as weak and comically irrelevant. When it was announced that Hillary Clinton would become a grandmother, opponents suggested she drop out of politics to stay home and knit for the baby. Nothing is a stronger cultural lightning rod than two needles and a ball of yarn.

But by Saturday night in the Big Apple, we were feeling our oats. We'd bent the hotel to our will. We had the waitstaff and bartenders and housekeepers trained. Do *not* touch the shawl that's blocking on the bedspread. Bring extra water to all the classrooms, and make sure it has lots of ice in it. When I say "Tanqueray and tonic," I mean *pronto*.

As we sprawled and knit and drank and talked in the lobby that evening, I noticed a disturbance in our midst. Newcomers were arriving, fancy people in suits and winter coats and furs. They walked in clusters, exerting a confidence that suggested they, not us, were the ones who owned the place.

They were oblivious to our signage, to our yarn displays, to our sprawl, just as most of the knitters were oblivious to them. I watched as a man with a big camera took pictures of the people shaking hands.

I'd gone to the lobby to meet Stephanie for dinner. She was surrounded by fans near a group of the newcomers. I joined her and glanced over at the fancy people. A distinguished older gentleman met my eye. I smiled and he gave me a wink.

I learned later that I'd just exchanged a smile with Willie Mays, the highest-ranking living player in baseball history. He was in town for the New York chapter of the Baseball Writers' Association of America's annual awards gala, which was taking place somewhere in the bowels of our hotel. *Sports Illustrated* would describe that evening's event as, with the exception of the All-Star Game, "the greatest assemblage of baseball stars in one place." And it was happening during the greatest assemblage of *knitting* stars in one place.

I wonder what a Knitting Writers' Association of America would look like. Where would we hold our banquets? And who would we invite? We have no shortage of designers, people with great skill in translating creative vision into numbers on paper. But we have far fewer capital-*W* Writers in the knitting world.

Stephanie would naturally be on the board, as would Debbie Stoller. June Hemmons Hiatt would get lifetime membership for her work on *The Principles of Knitting*. Of course, posthumous nods would be made to Richard Rutt for his *A History of Handknitting* and Elizabeth Zimmermann for, well, everything she did. Novelists Ann Hood and Debbie Macomber, they, too, would be card-carrying members. Maybe I'd try to pull strings and get historian Laurel Thatcher Ulrich an honorary membership for her inspiring work, *The Age of Homespun*.

That's still only six living people, not including myself. Forget the Hilton, we could just take a table at a diner for our meetings. Maybe a diner like the one I went to for lunch the next afternoon.

I'd been teaching for so long that my brain was starting to get fuzzy, usually a sign that I should get out and take a walk. I headed away from the hotel as fast as my feet would carry me, down to West 47th Street to the nearest greasy old-school diner I could find. A TV on the wall was blaring the Fox News Channel, and a man a few stools down from me at the counter made a grunt of disapproval. I turned and smiled.

"Of course they're playing that garbage," he muttered, "their offices are on the other side of that wall." I noticed all the framed, signed head-shots on the wall—all of Fox News celebrities.

We started talking and he asked where I was from. When I said Maine, he launched into an inventory of all the cruises he'd taken up the coast with his wife. "We've taken, let's see now, seventeen cruises," he said. "We've done New England, the Caribbean, the Panama Canal, Europe . . ." He was counting on his fingers now. When I confessed I'd never taken one, he started advising me on which cruise lines were better, had better crews, better ships, less likelihood of running aground or giving you dysentery.

My only clue that this wasn't just an old guy who loved cruises and wanted his corned-beef hash extra crunchy was the fact that the waitstaff all referred to him by his last name, reverently adding "Mister" before they said it.

"There's my sound guy!" He suddenly greeted someone over my shoulder. "Come on over here, buddy," he added, motioning a young, friendly-looking man over to the empty seat between us. Introductions were made. They worked on a Broadway show that had just opened at a nearby theater. This was their quiet lunchtime hangout, safely hidden from the cheesecake-seeking tourists of Times Square.

Just then, another man came in, dapper and extremely handsome, with a spring in his step and that kind of inexplicable charisma that makes you want to stare. They introduced him as the star of the show, a dancer who'd also made a name for himself on a very popular television show I didn't watch. I'd never heard his name before.

"So, what brings you to New York?" asked the star.

I wanted to say I was rehearsing at Carnegie Hall, or giving a reading somewhere, perhaps recording a new album. I knew that the moment I told the truth, that I was there for a knitting conference of all things, their faces would fall. We'd have a repeat of the elevator scenes, the telltale awkward silence before they could find a way to beat a retreat.

But then something unexpected happened. As soon as I told them the truth, the sound man broke into a smile, swiveled on his stool, and lifted up his pant leg to reveal the cuff of a perfectly executed, clearly handknitted sock.

"I told my mom, I don't want any other gifts from now on. Just socks!"

PERKY SKEINS AND
FAST CARS: Los Angeles

LOS ANGELES, the city of dreams, where palm trees and beautiful people bask in sunshine 365 days a year. With the exception of maybe UGG boots, LA isn't known for its wool culture. It's not a place you'd expect to find knitters in great number.

But in 2011, following on the heels of its successful premiere in New York City, Vogue Knitting LIVE extended its reach to Los Angeles. It was a test of how our grounded, joyful reality would rub up against the forever-young illusion of Southern California. As a Mainer, I welcomed a chance to see the sun one last time in September before winter took hold. That's one among many reasons I and almost 100 other teachers, staffers, and volunteers said yes to the invitation.

Our home for the three days of the show was the crescent-shaped Hyatt Century Plaza hotel. The building is pure 1960s architecture, with balconies running along each floor like ruffles on a flamenco dancer's skirt. It was built, along with the rest of Century City, on 180 acres of former 20th Century Fox Studios back lot. After opening in 1966, the hotel immediately became a hub for Hollywood's glamor set—and it remained that way, give or take, until the fall of the Berlin Wall.

Fast-forward to 2008, when new owners tried to put the (by now) tired building out of its misery. Local preservation groups sprang to action, and eventually demolition plans were scrapped and a kinder, gentler renovation got underway.

Just nineteen months after the hotel was rescued, we knitters took over. Our taxis and shuttles had to squeeze by a row of glimmering Ferraris that were parked in front of the hotel for the duration of the weekend. Men in suits swooped down to welcome us. They had earpieces with curly translucent cords tucked under their collars. Occasionally, one of them would mumble into his lapel. Although they were mostly summonsing cars from the valet garage, they conjured up images of Secret Service men during presidential visits. Presidents Johnson and Nixon stayed here, and Ronald Reagan was such a frequent guest that the hotel was nicknamed the "Western White House" while he was in office.

But that was long ago. For this brief weekend, knitters would be the guests of honor. It was a difficult dichotomy to grasp at first. The polished-marble, shimmering-glass lobby seemed filled with glamorous women tottering in impossibly high-heeled shoes, their bare legs looking Photo-shopped even in broad daylight. They wore no wool, and their bags—barely big enough for lipstick and a cell phone—held no yarn. But glancing deeper into the lobby, I spotted the beginnings of the knitter invasion.

A funny thing happens when more than one knitter gathers in a public place. A solo knitter, presuming she is a woman, quickly fades into the backdrop like a potted palm or a quietly nursing mother. We are a cultural metaphor for invisibility—something Agatha Christie knew quite well when she gave Miss Marple her needles and yarn. What better cloak of invisibility from which to observe the evil-doings of the world? A single knitter is shorthand for "nothing to see here, move on."

But when knitters gather, we become incongruously conspicuous. We are a species that other people aren't used to seeing in flocks, like a cluster of Corgis, a dozen Elvis impersonators waiting for the elevator.

Here in our Century Plaza lobby, the flocking had already begun. The hotel's well-oiled social machine of seeing-and-being-seen began to sputter as passersby slowed and did double takes. Here, just steps from Hollywood, were regular people doing something joyfully regular, and none of them gave a damn what the rest of the world thought.

The event was smaller in scale than its East Coast counterpart, with just over fifty classes and lectures. But the roster sparkled with the likes of Meg Swansen, Nicky Epstein, and Sally Melville. Deborah Norville, avid knitter and host of *Inside Edition*, was on hand for photos and auto-graphs. A "Beginner's Lounge" was staffed by Vickie Howell, then host of the DIY channel's *Knitty Gritty*. A marketplace brought more than seventy-five vendors, big and small, to town.

I was there to teach my classes about the properties of fiber and yarn construction. At that time, my focus was squarely on wool. Southern California not having a big wool culture, my classes were small. They were held in converted guest rooms, skirted tables replacing beds, with only headboards (permanently affixed to the walls) to remind us of the room's primary function. One class had just three brave, brilliant students. We sat in a tiny room overlooking the bottom of an air shaft, and I gave them the best class of my life.

At lunchtime, the more adventurous among us bypassed the lines at the hotel restaurant, slipping by the gleaming Ferraris to dodge LA traffic and visit the glitzy outdoor mall across the way. Shops opened directly onto terraces with padded sofas and lounge chairs in convenient clusters. Everything was open to the elements. This being September, heaters had already been wheeled out and set to use. No wonder the city comes to a standstill when it rains.

The glassed-in luxury food court was mobbed. I picked a ramen vendor and met up with Lorna's Laces owner Beth Casey and her husband, both of whom hail from Chicago. We sat outside and let ourselves get sunburned, as East Coasters tend to do when in the sudden presence of sun.

Our serenity was gradually interrupted by cleaning staff struggling to keep ahead of the pigeons. Each time a table was vacated, it was a race to see who would descend first. The pigeons always won, wings flapping madly as they scattered fried rice and pizza crusts and bits of wilted lettuce onto the pavement.

Afterward, I slipped into Bloomingdale's and briefly toyed with a wallet that cost more than my entire paycheck for the weekend. Then it was back to my hotel room for a quick nap before more workshops, more demonstrations, more laps around the marketplace. From my balcony, I could see glistening rows of bodies next to the pools below. Over the parking garages and office buildings in front of me was a flat sea of West Los Angeles. Somewhere to my left, barely a mile away, were the rooftops under which Fox Studios made its magic.

Different magazines have different focuses, some technique, others easy beginner projects. Over the years, *Vogue Knitting* has always put fashion trends first, showcasing knitted works of design icons like Perry Ellis, Calvin Klein, and Missoni. Fittingly, on Saturday night after all the workshops had let out, we gathered under a Hollywood-style tent for a gala evening featuring a presentation by Kaffe Fassett followed by a fashion show.

I'd like to tell you how memorable it was, how much I enjoyed Kaffe's talk and how inspired I was by the garments on display, but the truth is that I arrived too late for a seat. I ended up ducking out a side door and joining friends for dinner. One of them, an Emmy-nominated hairstylist for television and film, was working on a popular TV show at the time. She regaled us with tales of what the real Hollywood world is like when the cameras aren't shooting. Somewhere between appetizers and entrees, a soprano appeared out of nowhere and began singing an aria. Our waiter leaned over and whispered, "Don't worry, they do this every week."

The show ended at 4:30 PM on Sunday, and the set was immediately dismantled, as if everyone had been waiting for the bell to announce quitting time. Posters were yanked down, the black velvet dressmaker's dummies stripped of their display handknits. Vendors packed up so quickly, some didn't even bother taping up their boxes or removing their nametags. They stood on the curb, in the shadow of those Ferraris, guarding their boxes while someone else ran to retrieve the cars.

I found a quiet chair in the lounge and pulled out my knitting. Some knitters lingered at other tables, too. We weren't getting quite as many stares now. When my handsome young waiter-slash-aspiring-actor delivered my gin and tonic, he pointed at my knitting. "There was a huge store set up over the weekend," he began, as if I'd missed the whole thing.

"Oh I know," I said. "It just closed. Everyone should be gone soon."

His face fell. "I saw some really cool stuff in there but I had to work my shift." He paused and looked around at another lingering knitter. "Do you think there are any stores around here where I could, like, you know . . . learn how to do that?"

NAKED LOPI: A Knitter's Journey to Iceland

I'D BEEN WARNED about the nudity. This was Iceland, after all, the land of Vikings and volcanic hot springs and Claudia Schiffer lookalikes. When you're five foot nine and weigh 115 pounds, with a perfect complexion and body unaffected by gravity, why wouldn't you want to strip naked and hop into a pool?

This little factoid had been so discretely tucked into an otherwise exciting weeklong itinerary of yarn fondling and sheep wrangling that I let myself forget it would happen, like that root canal you avoid by chewing on the other side.

It was thus, bleary-eyed and optimistic, that I landed in Iceland one bright September morning just as the sun was peeking over the horizon. Beyond passport control, I met the outstretched arms of Ragnheiður Eiríksdóttir—better known to American knitters by her nickname, Ragga. For several years, this charismatic knitting instructor and designer, also a psychiatric nurse, popular columnist, radio and television commentator, and sex educator, had been bringing a steady stream of knitters to her island. At last, after more than a year of waiting, it was my turn.

Soon enough we were on the road, the intense morning sunrise illuminating the cracks in Ragga's windshield. A tiny handknitted sweater dangled from her rearview mirror, the Icelandic version of fuzzy dice or a pine-scented air freshener.

The airport is about thirty miles southwest of the capital city of Reykjavík. There is no town, really. Just an airport and open space and that feeling of having landed on a remote outpost. Nearby, I spotted a bleak clump of boxy buildings—imagine IKEA had designed 1970s prisons—that turned out to be an old NATO base. When it was decommissioned, the airstrip became the new airport.

Nearly half of the island is composed of lava fields, and the road into Reykjavík takes you smack dab through them. The smooth strip of Tarmac runs over what looks like a pan of brownies that someone tried to cut before they cooled. Here and there, a dusting of DayGlo-green moss provides contrast.

There was no, "aha!" moment when a cityscape unfolded, when I knew I'd arrived in Reykjavík. Just a gradual increase in traffic, more signs, more buildings. Roundabouts became traffic lights. To our left, a bacon processor adjacent to a mayonnaise manufacturer, or, as Ragga called it, the BLT factory. Hills of tidy, well-tended housing developments appeared on the right, a slightly cheerier, more verdant version of the Daly City you pass on your way into San Francisco.

Finally, I spotted a tall, jagged steeple. It looked like a cross between a Mormon temple and the ice caves in the original Superman movie. This Lutheran church is the largest in Iceland and is the country's sixth-tallest architectural structure, commissioned in 1937 and completed in 1986. When you're in Reykjavík, you quickly learn to orient yourself by it.

Ragga told me it was the Hallgrímskirkja.

"Could you repeat that?" I asked.

"Hallgrímskirkja," she said more slowly.

I tried to repeat the sounds that just came out of her mouth. She laughed, shook her head, and repeated, "Hall ... grím ... skir ... kja ..."

I have a good ear, and I'd rather assumed that I'd be able to memorize a few key words to ease my way into conversation. I was wrong. Icelandic is a gorgeous, rich, complex, utterly impenetrable mash-up of Old Norse sounds harking back to the island's first settlers in the ninth century. Vaguely familiar vowels and consonants are punctuated by guttural sounds, faint whistles, and trilly tongue flutters, sounds you didn't even know the human mouth was capable of making. Written, it looks like a cat walked across the keyboard.

In the end, I would spend eight days attempting "thank you" (þakka þér, don't make me try to say it again) without ever getting a nod. The closest approval I got was with a phrase that means, roughly, "I am a dumb tourist."

There had been some apprehension leading up to the visit, mostly because Ragga had been MIA for weeks. I was left not quite sure of where I'd stay, or whether she'd be there to meet me, or whether we'd have a tour at all. At the last minute, she swooped into our inboxes with words of reassurance, but I still didn't know where I'd be staying. In a hotel, on a couch, sharing a bed with one of my students?

But the news was good. Ragga showed me up to an apartment on the top floor of her building, just steps from the Superman church. Every fifteen minutes on the dot, the bells chimed, usually to remind us we were going to be late for something. Ragga's internal clock has no hurry to it.

The interior hallway gave off that telltale musty fragrance of mixed lives. Strange spices, oils, perfumes, and another smell I finally recognized as feet. Each doorway had a small rack for shoes. Some were empty, others heaped. I imagined the boots piled high in winter. On each landing, lace-curtained windows offered a glimpse into the backyard world of rarely used decks, balconies, and yards.

It was early yet, not even 8:00 AM. After dropping off my luggage, we walked around the corner and sat on a bench outside Ragga's favorite café, which was still a few minutes shy of opening. At that hour, it was mostly groggy schoolchildren, groggy parents, and cats. Lots of cats, gazing at us from beneath parked cars, sunning themselves in windowsills, trotting down the sidewalk, defiantly twitching their tails at us. Cats are everywhere in Reykjavík. The other thing I learned while on that bench was that Ragga *didn't* have persistent flatulence, it was the abundant sulfur in the city's water. All of Reykjavík smells, gently, discretely, undeniably of rotten eggs.

The leaves were just beginning to turn, and the air had that distinct back-to-school chill. By December, they'd have just four hours and seven minutes of daylight—versus the sixteen hours we would be enjoying. I found myself entertaining a thought I'd have again and again during my time in Iceland: What must this place be like in the winter? I pictured the streets shrouded in darkness and snow. It must be the perfect place to go after a bad break-up, to hunker down and wallow. Then summer comes, and by July they face the opposite problem: a sun that never truly sets. It just goes into dusk mode for a few hours before popping back up over the horizon.

By now, the café was open, so we wandered inside. The menu was an enigma. I did not see anything that could, if you removed the dots and squiggles, be guessed to be "cappuccino." Prices made no sense, either, what with 1 króna equaling approximately $0.00886 US dollars. I picked one at random and asked Ragga if it was any good. "Sure! Yeah!" she said. The price was 500 krónur. My brother had warned me how expensive Iceland was. I'd never paid 500 *anything* for coffee before, but my jetlag-addled brain was incapable of doing the math.

We sat at a table made out of an old treadle sewing machine. Ragga pulled over a tray of nail polish the café made available to customers. I'd seen it on other tourists' Instagram feeds. She sloshed some mustard yellow on her short nails while we waited for our order. Music was playing, and every once in a while, someone would saunter over to a turntable to switch the record. We went through Talking Heads, Debbie Harry, then the Beatles. I watched long legs with colorful tights and impossibly high-heeled ankle boots—the official footwear for most women in the city—bob up and down to the music at other tables.

These people looked nothing like the ones I'm used to seeing in my neighborhood, even at my favorite indie coffeehouse. These were gorgeous, elegant, finely crafted human specimens. Soft-spoken and visually dramatic, the women looked like Nobel prize-winning Swedish supermodels, the men like Viking reenactors, but in skinny jeans and Converse high-tops. No matter who it was, no matter how shaggy his or her hair or geometric his or her glasses, everyone was wearing wool. Not the fine Italian stuff, either, but thick Icelandic wool knit into bulky sweaters.

The sweater is called a *lopapeysa*, and it's a national treasure. Everyone has at least one, from the baggage handlers to the garbage collectors, mothers and hipsters and old folk alike. I didn't see a dog in such a sweater, but that doesn't mean they weren't there.

While it'd be much more romantic to think that the *lopapeysa* has been around since the Viking days, this iconic style is actually a twentieth-century invention. Nobody knows exactly how it started, but this thick sweater with colorful patterning around the yoke (and sometimes waist and sleeve) gained popularity in the 1950s, about the same time my grandparents first set foot on the island. My grandma went berserk with the stuff, jamming her suitcase with finished sweaters and pounds of Icelandic wool yarn, with which she knit her grandchildren wonderfully rugged, scratchy *lopapeysur* (the plural for *lopapeysa*). She wore one of these cardigans every day, rain or shine, no matter the season. It was such a permanent part of her wardrobe that the cuffs had to be darned repeatedly to compensate for her compulsive fidgeting. I almost brought one with me to Iceland, but I couldn't quite bear to risk losing it. The *lopapeysa* took on a renewed symbol of national pride following Iceland's economic collapse in 2008. By the time I got there in 2012, they were everywhere.

Nails dry and fully caffeinated, Ragga and I embarked on a walking tour of town. Along the narrow roads of Laugavegur and Bankastræti, we zigzagged back and forth from window to window. Ragga seemed to know everyone we passed. "He's my cousin," she'd say, waving to a man across the street. "We go way back," she'd say about someone else. "She's a famous fashion designer," she'd tell me as she pointed to a woman we just met entering a building, or "That's my ex-husband's sister." I joked that she was like the mayor of Reykjavík. "No, he's way cooler," she said. "He was in our last Gay Pride parade, in full drag."

The cars seemed to have no agenda. They slowed, like sheep, to let us cross. I could only imagine how baffled an Icelandic pedestrian would be upon encountering drivers, honking, selfish, impatient, in one of the United States' capital cities.

I asked where we were in relation to home, and Ragga pointed to a street sign nearby, apparently our street. It said "Skólavörðustígur." I didn't even bother to ask her to repeat it, nor did I bother to try and write it down. I memorized the first part, "Skóla," and then replaced the rest with what would become my standard banter, a bad imitation of the Swedish chef from the Muppets.

You don't realize how highly keyed your barometer of danger is until you go to a place like Iceland. I only saw one police officer the whole time

I was there. Graffiti did cover walls and fences, but it was always a bright and colorful artistic adornment. The few pierced youths I passed, walking four across on the sidewalk, still stepped aside to let me get by.

Ragga left me at a market on our street to stock my kitchen with provisions. You can tell so much about a place by its grocery stores. In Iceland, the biggest difference may be in the bottled water aisle—by which I mean you won't find one. Buying bottled water in Iceland would be like traveling to Poland Springs, Maine, and refusing to drink from the tap.

Instead, I picked up a tetra pak of Mjölk for my tea, daydreamed in the baking aisle, and gaped at the selection of Skyr. This decadent Icelandic concoction claims to be strained yogurt but tastes for all the world like unadulterated crème fraîche. Having already gotten hooked on it in the States, I snagged an obscene amount, just because I could.

I'd come to Iceland for an eight-day trip of a lifetime billed as the Clara Parkes Iceland Experience. What it really meant was that I'd be teaching two three-hour workshops on yarn and wool, Ragga would teach one three-hour workshop on the *lopapeysa*, and then the group would pack up our bags, head into the country, and be tourists together, collectively fondling yarn and gawking at sheep. We were sixteen people total, including Ragga and her cherubic assistant, Fanney. I knew two people on the tour from the *Knitter's Review* Retreat. Everyone else was new to me.

We hailed mostly from the United States, with a demographic leaning toward an over-fifty crowd. We were women mostly, and many of us were grappling with empty nests, recent widowhood, spinsterhood, and Peggy Lee's eternal question, "Is that all there is?" Iceland was a major line item on each of our bucket lists.

Everyone else in the group bunked together at a hostel down the hill from my apartment. Sets of strangers had been tasked with duking it out: Who got the real bed, who would sleep on the couch, and who could pretend to be least bothered by the choice? Nanci, a New Jersey expat living in Toronto, took one look at the accommodations and demanded that Ragga find her a proper hotel.

Our workshops were to be held a short walk away at the KEX, a waterfront hangout that just happened to be one of the top hostels of the world. The carefully rumpled lobby was a Grand Central Station of hipster—just the previous week Patti Smith and Russell Crowe had given an impromptu concert in the library. The day after I arrived, Ragga took me there for lunch before we met the group for the first time. She glanced over my shoulder, smiled, and whispered that members of the Icelandic band Sigur Rós were there giving an interview to the foreign press.

In the company of the right person, someone as knowledgeable and connected as Ragga for example, it's possible to feel like you've slipped right into the fabric of the city. They love tourists in Iceland, especially since they have played such an important role in the rebuilding of the economy. Just don't try to move there permanently. Iceland has erected very high, costly, and time-consuming barriers to permanent immigration including, but not limited to, a complete FBI criminal background check. As traditionally difficult as immigration has been, cultural assimilation is even harder. My friend Anna was born in a tiny Iceland town, moved to the United States as a child, and was completely rejected when she tried to return as a teenager. As devastating as that experience was for her, she is still fiercely proud of her Icelandic heritage.

Keeping intruders out of paradise is nothing new. My friend Bettina told me the same thing about South Carolina. "They love you down there, they really do," she said, "as long as you don't move there." Come to think of it, I've heard that about parts of Maine, too.

Our group quickly warmed to one another in that way strangers do when thrown together. Characters emerged. Like Kelly, a short, freckled redhead with razor-sharp intellect and an infectious laugh, who became our unofficial legal counsel. She'd retired to Arizona after a career in Los Angeles prosecuting murderers and drug lords. We took turns testing theories on her, trying to concoct the perfect crime for which you'd never get caught.

Playing Hardy to Kelly's Laurel was the tall, slender Helen from Rhode Island, long-ago divorced and recently retired and always, *always* in a good mood. She'd slink away and photograph things none of us had found, triumphantly returning to show us her latest windowsill vignettes, cats, croissants from the local French bakery, and details of passing *lopapeysur*. Kelly and Helen were plunked in a threesome with Lou, an avid handspinner from Evansville, Illinois, who Skyped with her cat every night.

Every group has its puppy, or pair of puppies, and ours were Kat and Frog, a young couple from Australia. This was their first major journey off their island, and their bright-eyed enthusiasm was contagious. Rarely have I ever been around two people who were more game for *anything*.

Their Australian accents were charmingly thick and chewy. I loved the way they said "Pith" instead of "Perth," "bick" instead of "back." Thwarted by Icelandic, I set about mimicking their accents instead.

Having already established her reputation as the Princess-and-the-Pea of our group, Nanci-from-Toronto-but-originally-from-New-Jersey surprised us by actually being quite game for anything, too.

On our last night in Reykjavík before leaving for the countryside, we were gathered at the KEX for dinner. Ragga had just finished giving Nanci directions to the famous hot dog stand where Bill Clinton ate (just before undergoing open-heart surgery) and where Anthony Bourdain filmed a late-night segment of *No Reservations*.

"Be sure to get the 'everything' hot dog," Ragga advised.

Nanci's eyes narrowed, "What's on it?"

"It has remoulade, it has mustard . . ."

Nanci interrupted, "No, no, *no mustard.*"

"It has ketchup . . ."

"No. Listen," she squared off. "I like my hot dogs split down the middle, with grill marks down the back . . ."

"Well, you will not get that hot dog in Iceland," Ragga smiled. "Yours will have crispy fried onions . . ."

Nanci perked up. "Like onion rings?"

"No. Like an onion that has been fried."

"Do they *have* onion rings?"

You could see Nanci struggling. At last, she shrugged. "Oh well, I'll try it anyway. Now exactly where is it again?"

Later that night, as I was finishing up my last class, there was a banging at the window. The chef had gone out for a smoke, glanced upward, and spotted the Northern Lights. This dazzling phenomenon is best viewed in the magnetic polar regions where it gets really, really dark at night—making Iceland prime viewing territory.

"Everyone, outside!" Ragga yelled. "Class dismissed!" We donned our coats, grabbed our cameras, and trotted out the door. Once our eyes had adjusted to the darkness, we saw magical wisps of Ghostbusters green in the sky.

I stayed up far too late that night, nose to my bedroom window, gazing at the green. It kept shifting shape. First it was fog, then distinct rays, then a giant bubble like a cartoon caption. I tried to Skype the sky back home to my partner, Clare, but my camera just couldn't capture it. Not even our cat was interested.

The next morning, it was time to leave the city, head north, and find some sheep. We trundled our suitcases to the street and boarded a narrow bus driven by Reynir, a stern and sullen young man with a baby face and the beginnings of a belly. He wore a dark jacket with the tour-bus company's insignia embroidered on it.

We were barely fifteen minutes out of Reykjavík when we made our first stop. Our destination was the town of Mosfellsbær and Ístex, which is to yarn what Willie Wonka's factory is to chocolate. The typical image of a spinning mill always seems to involve ancient brick buildings perched next to a rushing river, but the Ístex mill—the largest mill in Iceland, and the one where nearly every skein of Icelandic yarn comes from—occupies a thoroughly modern box of a building.

The original mill, Álafoss, went bankrupt in 1991 after ninety-five years of operation. Three of the original employees bought the company (and now share it with a fourth owner) and changed its name to Ístex. They retain 50-percent ownership, and the other half of the company is owned by the Icelandic Sheep Farmers Association, which currently numbers 1,800 members and represents nearly all sheep farmers on the island.

We walked down tidy beech-colored hallways of an IKEA-styled office building, not quite sure how it related to the manufacturing of yarn. And then through a set of heavy doors that led into the site we wanted to see: the mill.

Here were the ancient machines, still operating with loud, mesmerizing precision. I had the feeling of watching a vintage B-52 bomber that's been carefully maintained in perfect working order, Singer Featherweights on a massive scale. Some of what we smelled wasn't wool at all but the grease necessary to keep all the moving parts lubricated.

We gazed, dumbfounded, at the bales of scoured Icelandic wool stacked from floor to ceiling. This represented the bulk of wool produced in Iceland. The average farm has between 300 and 500 sheep. Multiply that times the 1,800 farms that sell their wool to Ístex every year, and you begin to get a sense of the scope of this operation. Of course, wool is just part of the sheep equation, the bigger and more profitable half being those Icelandic lamb chops being sold at your local Whole Foods.

But here, we were too busy gazing at the mountain of Icelandic wool bales. A nearby bale had been cut open and a tuft of wool was sticking out. When our guide turned away, Ragga grabbed the clump, yanked it from the bale, and shoved it in my raincoat pocket. In one moment, I'd gone from stupid tourist to felon. "You'll want this for later," she said.

Our circuit through the mill followed the natural order of yarn production, as everything had been laid out so that the fibers could be moved sequentially (and efficiently) from one machine and process to the next. We watched giant steel hooks lift dyed fleece from their tanks, still dripping. We gazed into the room in which different colors of fiber are blown and tossed about. Many of the Lopi colors are heathers, which means that what we see as blue might actually be an artful blend of light and dark blue, purple, perhaps a dusting of red. That mixing room is where the color magic begins. Next, the mixed fibers are transported to massive carding machines that tease the fibers apart into a smooth sheet of blended beauty that is, at last, peeled off into narrow strips, rubbed together, wound onto long spools. These spools are then lifted off the card and moved to spinning frames, where they are stretched and twisted into true yarn. The barely spun Plötulopi doesn't even go to the spinning frame, the fibers get pulled off the spool and sold as-is.

The pièce de résistance was a new investment, an amazing robotic machine that winds the yarn into tidy balls and plops them into little cradles on a conveyor belt, where padded mechanical "hands" reach down and give them a squeeze. Another set of mechanical hands retrieves each ball and wraps a thick paper label snugly around its belly. At the end, the skeins pass by conveyor belt to a woman who slips them neatly into clear plastic bags and tucks them in boxes that are shipped to yarn stores around the world. With almost no exception, if you buy yarn from Iceland, whether it's labeled Plötulopi, Álafosslopi, Bulkylopi, Léttlopi, or Einband, it comes from here.

Not everything had been mechanized at the mill. Near the end of our tour, we reached a woman standing at high table not too far from the robotic wonder. Her task was to twist finished hanks by hand, slide paper labels over them, and then stack them in a tidy pile. There she stood, government-mandated ear protection firmly in place, patiently doing one of the world's most tedious jobs while we all smiled and took videos of her graceful, well-practiced motions, giving her the universal thumbs-up sign.

Primed and ready to spend, our next stop was the Álafoss factory store, located along the Varmá River in the older part of Mosfellsbær. Here, we finally had the picturesque old mill building beside the gurgling stream, with creaky wood floors and haunting black-and-white photos of how things used to be. A mill has stood here since 1896. Today, it is strictly a place for tourists to come and part with their money. Our bus parked in a lot next to a nondescript building that happened to house the studio for the same band that I'd spotted at the KEX earlier in the week—Sigur Rós.

Once across the street and inside the factory store, everyone went nuts. We'd been given a discount on already inexpensive yarns, and people stumbled back to the bus with giant bags that had to be stuffed in the luggage bays. I, however, was smug. *I've seen enough yarn in my lifetime*, I thought. *I am above buying more just because I'm at a factory outlet and have been given a discount.* Just to prove my point, I made it out with a single set of rosewood circular needles.

From here, we quieted down for our two-hour ride north to the

Snæfellsnes Peninsula. Our road took us right along the coast before dipping down, down, down, 500 feet beneath the Hvalfjörður fjord. The two-lane tunnel ran for more than three miles. After a few light jokes about claustrophobia, Reynir mumbled something and Ragga pulled out her microphone. "Our driver tells me this tunnel was closed briefly last year after a truck exploded." For the first time, he smiled.

Ears popping, we ascended into a wilder, more remote landscape. Jagged mountain peaks shot up on our right, their soft, green sides sloping elegantly to a frothy coastline on our left, the landscape of a Dior gown. We'd passed the outer limits of the North Atlantic and were now gazing at the Denmark Strait.

Suddenly, we turned off the road and into the parking lot of the Icelandic equivalent of a suburban Safeway. "Okay, folks!" Ragga announced over the PA system, "This is it! Our last grocery store for quite a while. If you'd like any snacks for the next few days, now's your time to get them."

We all dutifully marched in, heads bowed against a brutal wind and the beginnings of rain. You'd think we were remote explorers preparing for a year in the outback the way we heaped our carts high with cookies and crackers and chips. Past the dried fruit I sauntered, eyeing the canned goods, the school supplies, the ... I stopped.

There, inside a regular old grocery store, was a complete yarn section. Not just a shelf or two, but shelves and racks and bins and an entire wall of every conceivable color and weight of Icelandic yarn, from the barely spun Plötulopi to the chunky Álafosslopi, from Bulkylopi to the lighter Léttlopi and lace-weight Einband.

This was identical to what I'd just left at the factory store. But something about the supermarket setting made me snap. The heathered colors were suddenly exquisite and irresistible. Right then, I decided I would knit a small blanket during this trip, something I could put on my lap while reminiscing about my time in Iceland. The ever-game Kat and Frog kept me company, augmenting their stashes with multiple shades of green for a project *they* would complete during their trip. (Only they actually did.)

"Did you *see* the yarn section?" we asked one another back on the bus, stowing our bags of cookies and drinks. Ragga smiled patiently.

"They had yarn!" we kept repeating in disbelief.

"In a grocery store!"

"I KNOW!"

The fact that the prices made no sense made the whole thing even more exciting. Unless you had a calculator or a gift for numbers, it was almost impossible to know exactly what you'd just spent. Everything seemed like a bargain *and* a splurge, we never quite knew.

We bounced our way up the peninsula, lulled to sleep by the *thwack, thwack, thwack* of the windshield wipers. Reynir's seat had a life of its own. Every time we hit a bump—which we did with increasing frequency—his seat would rise high, then let out a slow hiss as it settled back down again.

Suddenly, a cry came from the back of the bus. "Sheeeeeeep!"

All eyes turned to see our very first, true, capital-*I* Icelandic sheep. Out there! In the wild! We pulled out our cameras. We *ooh*ed and *aah*ed. This was why we'd come.

The Icelandic sheep is a rarity in the modern world. Its genetics can be traced to the original sheep brought to the island by early Viking settlers in the ninth century. Back then, we relied on sheep for everything—milk, meat, wool, and skin alike. They grew varied coats with fibers ranging from the fineness of silk to long, rugged strands best used for ropes. Everything came from these sheep. Even the sails on Viking ships were made from this wool, spun by hand on a spindle.

While the rest of the world set about "improving" their sheep breeds from the late 1700s onward, to grow bigger bodies and softer, brighter wool, Iceland's sheep remained untouched. Smaller than the average bulked-up commercial sheep, their coats still grow two distinct kinds of fiber. Thick, long rugged fibers are called *tog*, and they act as I-beams in the yarn, making it strong and durable. The short, exquisitely fine fibers are called *thel*, and they act as blown-in insulation, making those strong and durable garments also extraordinarily warm. Icelandic sheep still produce coats in a gorgeous array of natural colors far beyond just brilliant white. Their overall lack of genetic meddling makes these sheep an eerily accurate time capsule to the ninth century, which, in turn, makes Iceland such a compelling tourist destination today.

A few minutes later, another cry, more clicking. Then another cry, and another, until the cry became a joke because the sheep, they were *everywhere*.

The landscape had become vast and rugged, with nothing but raised roads and irrigation ditches to suggest where one property might end and another begin. Regardless of where we looked or whose property it may have been, we found sheep. Everywhere. These furry skin tags on the landscape, plump little marshmallows dropped from on high, upon closer inspection they all revealed themselves to be sheep. There seemed to be no rhyme or reason to where they were roaming or how they managed to get there.

Like loitering teenagers, the sheep stood alone or in small clusters. The more remote the terrain, the warier they were of our approach. They'd wait until we were within grabbing distance to turn and run, their wooly behinds going rumpety-bumpety-bump away from us, until they felt it safe to stop, turn around, and stare.

Sheep may be among the most common animals on the island today, but when the early Vikings arrived, they also brought goats. Eventually they realized that they needed a fattier diet than the goats provided, so sheep gained favor. But the goats never quite left. Today, their biggest predator is the angry farmer who doesn't appreciate having his hay bales torn open and devoured.

One woman is doing her best to preserve and grow Iceland's native goat population. Her name is Jóhanna, and we reached her Háafell farm just before lunch. Her herd has the oldest native goat genes in all of Nordic Europe, dating back to those same early Viking settlers. Not only do these goats provide meat and milk, but they also grow—as does their cashmere cousin the *Capra hircus laniger*—a delicate undercoat of extraordinarily warm, fine fibers. The herd isn't nearly large enough yet to provide fibers for yarn production, but she hopes one day it will.

After a brief walk in the pasture, where Helen disappeared yet again to snap the best photographs, we assembled in a low cinderblock building for lunch. Jóhanna had set out a pretty table of cold cuts, thin slices of hearty black bread, slabs of butter, small chunks of goat's milk cheese, stacks of cookies, yogurt, and a pitcher of goat's milk, fresh from the udder. A tiny vase held roses from her garden.

I watched our group politely bypass the cold cuts and make a beeline for the butter. We were like termites with the butter, devouring every ounce of it wherever we went. I don't know if it was empirically better or if it was the allure of being away from home and throwing all dietary rules out the window, but the butter in Iceland *tasted* better, we'd all agreed on this.

We also doubled up on the chocolate-covered digestive biscuits. Jane from Seattle poured me a tall glass of lukewarm goat's milk, which I accepted with a smile that concealed deep regret. That morning's breakfast of dried fish dredged in butter, and the subsequent bouncy road, had left me feeling a little off.

Shooing flies off our plates, we listened to Ragga translate for Jóhanna. She didn't have a licensed commercial kitchen, so she couldn't sell any of the milk or cheese we were eating. Instead, she used the goat's milk for her own homemade skincare products. Which meant that after lunch, we dutifully lined up to buy jars of creams and lotions and salves that promised to restore our youthful complexions.

Back in the bus for another hour of bouncing, we reached a tiny home-based shop run by some old friends of Ragga's. Ducking as I passed through the small entryway, I sniffed a musty smell and glanced to my right to see something white in a bowl of brilliant red. A freshly severed sheep's head. They carved buttons from the horns, and I didn't ask what would happen to the rest.

We were shown their handcrafted wares, things like beautiful felted wool slippers and the carved sheephorn buttons. Fingering the wad of fiber in my pocket, I glanced at Ragga. She raised an eyebrow and pointed under a low shelf at the end of the room. My pulse quickened.

This farm participated in a small fiber cooperative that's little known outside of Iceland. Instead of selling their wool to Ístex, they pool it together and ship it to the same scouring plant that Ístex uses, but with different scouring instructions. They prefer to keep the water at a lower temperature, helping preserve more of the natural oils in the wool. I suspect Ístex has its fibers scoured at the temperature it does because they understand, probably rightly, that mainstream consumers aren't as enamored of the smell of sheep as knitters are. But it was impossible to deny that these lightly scoured fibers had a much more tender, succulent feel while retaining that telltale sheep fragrance. The fibers are then spun by Ístex into Plötulopi-styled yarn, which each member of the cooperative is allowed to sell.

Plötulopi is as close to knitting with a sheep as you can get. Its barely twisted, wisplike strands of fiber are usually held together in pairs to knit a garment. On its own, the yarn may be fragile, but as soon as it's knit up, you have a fabric that wears like steel. The other Icelandic yarns are presented in more conventional skeins or hanks, but Plötulopi comes right off the carding machine in disks or "cakes."

Beneath the counter that day, they had just a few cakes of brilliant white. The rest were a heathered gray, chocolate brown, and a relatively rare jet-black. In another room, they had large mesh bags of scoured, un-spun roving for sale. Happier than a pig in swill, I returned to the bus and stuffed my own bags in the luggage hold. To be fair, I *had* told the others why this yarn was so special, and I didn't grab it all.

The sun was about to set as we finally pulled into our hostel for the night. The squat cinderblock structure stood within roar's distance of the ocean. We looked up just in time to catch a rainbow spanning the entire sky, uninterrupted, from mountains to sea. A second rainbow appeared inside the bigger one.

Tucked into my narrow twin bed, I slept well that night. All around me, the comforting sounds of a hostel: the opening and closing of doors, hushed voices, footsteps on linoleum. Our muddy boots were neatly lined up on mats outside each door. Rain battered the roof all night. The wind huffed and it puffed, but it did not succeed in blowing us down.

Over breakfast the next morning, Helen from Rhode Island got it in her head that she wanted to ride one of Iceland's famous, pony-sized horses while she was here. She'd looked it all up on her iPad. She had the name of the place, the times, the fees, all of it. She just needed Ragga's assistant, Fanney, to make the call.

"Would anyone else like to go horseback riding?" came the question as Fanney pulled out her phone. What the hell, I raised my hand.

And so a smaller group of us piled into the bus and headed up the road a few miles to a horse farm. Beautiful little Icelandic horses were saddled and brought to us in a barn that was cleaner than most people's houses. One by one, we were led to our horse and helped onto it.

"Mine is moving!" cried Nanci from her horse. "Are they supposed to move?"

Two steps out of the barn, Nanci declared she was done. "I'm not ready for this!" And it was a good thing she did get off, because a few minutes later, passing through jaw-droppingly stunning scenery, someone made the mistake of suggesting that we go into a trot. Now, normal horses have just three gaits: walk, trot, and gallop. But the Icelandic horse breed has two additional gaits, *tölt* and *skeið*. While the *tölt* is allegedly very smooth and comfortable, it's also known for its sudden acceleration. And we weren't going into a mere trot, no. We were going into a *tölt*.

"Ready?" came the call from up front. My horse moved and I flew high into the air, feet out of the stirrups, butt out of the saddle. Only by some miracle did the saddle and stirrups return to greet me on the way down. Another leap, another miraculous save, over and over again, until—*thank God*—we slowed to a walk. Nobody else seemed to be in any state of distress. They were all smiling, relaxed, reliving childhood dreams of riding their own ponies off into the sunset.

Of course, I'd been given the horse with an eating disorder. While the other horses sauntered along just fine, mine wanted to stop at every bush, every bit of remotely edible brush. At first I did as told and yanked him back up, spurring him forward. Then I decided to strike a deal with him. "Okay, fella, I'll let you eat this stuff if you promise not to kill me before this ride is over. Do we have a deal?"

Apparently he listened, because an hour and three jarring and perilous tölts later, he safely deposited me back at the stable. But the day's adventure was far from over. After a quick stop to retrieve the rest of the group, including one person who was refusing to come out of her room (Ragga's training as a psych nurse came in handy), we hit the road again, this time for a remote field up the road. There, locals had assembled around a large, splintery wooden pen. They stood and chatted while, inside, hundreds of nervous sheep wondered what was going to happen next.

In Iceland, the sheep are allowed to wander as far and high as their hooves will take them during the summer months. All too soon, September rolls around and the farmers must retrieve their sheep. They're rounded up, herded down the slopes, and ushered into these penned areas no bigger than a city house lot. Each sheep is identified by a number on its ear tag and sent back to its home for winter.

This annual tradition of rounding up, sorting, and sending sheep home is called *réttir*, and it's why we'd come. There were no introductions, we just walked up to the pen, exchanged shy smiles, and stood.

Our task was to go inside and start "catching" sheep, which I assure you sounds far easier than it actually is. We were to grab their horns, raise a leg over their (sometimes dangerously high) backs, and straddle them tight while reading the number on their ear tags, finding someone who knew where that sheep went, and then escorting the reluctant sheep over to that pen.

Réttir is for neighbors, family, and friends. Our tour bus was an anomaly, a gently accepted intrusion into a local ritual. People perched on the rails and talked in clusters. Toddlers were lifted into the pen and walked around by their parents. Children caught the smaller ones. More experienced farmers did the task with panache, often grabbing a single horn and straddling the sheep so swiftly that it didn't realize what had happened. We were perhaps slightly less graceful, but we caught on quickly and did our part.

I hadn't been looking forward to this portion of the trip. I did not want to participate in traumatizing the animals. (Yes, I eat meat. I realize the hypocrisy.) But upon closer examination, there didn't appear to be any real damage. This was simply sorting. The sheep were not violent or mean, nor were the people. The animals protested, we asserted, and eventually everyone got squared away. I'll confess it felt unexpectedly pleasant to interact with the animals in such a physical way, to touch "living wool" while gazing into the eyes of the creature growing it.

I went for the shorter ones, lest a taller sheep take me for a ride. I also picked the ones with horns, for the same reason you'd choose a bicycle with handlebars instead of one without. I learned quickly that if you didn't hold the horns firmly with both hands, the sheep would wiggle their heads side to side, digging their horns into your thighs.

The overnight rain had made the ground muddy and slippery, and occasionally I had to stop and catch my breath. A few of us had already taken tumbles. "I am really, really sorry about this," I said to a particularly frisky young guy while I rubbed his cheek. "I promise, all I'm trying to do is get you over there. . . ." (I pointed, and I swear he looked.) "Once I do, it'll be over." They had very intelligent eyes. I knew they were sizing us up, too, figuring out which of us they could outrun.

The whole scene was like an Iceland tourist commercial. As if on cue, a beautiful young girl and her handsome father appeared on horseback and began giving friends rides. A cluster of equally beautiful people stood against one fence, colorful patterned *lopapeysa* after *lopapeysa* on adults and children alike. These walking advertisements for Iceland were, in fact, local sheep farmers and their families. One particularly tall, slender blonde woman drew our attention. She was breathtakingly beautiful, a dead ringer for Heidi Klum. Helen from Rhode Island sauntered over to snap a picture and reported back with a satisfied whisper, "She's wearing *makeup*."

We were too shy to approach people directly or ask to see their sweaters up close, so we teamed up to do walk-by shots of different sweaters. "You do the front of the yoke," we agreed, "and I'll go from behind to get the back detail." And so, across multiple cameras, we managed to capture the most memorable designs on display that afternoon.

As the day wound down, it was time to return the sheep to their farms. A few were loaded onto the backs of trucks, but most were sent home in a much simpler way: The farmer and his family lined up outside the gate, creating a long sort of human tunnel to direct the stampede. They opened the door, and out the sheep went, running rumpety-bumpety-bump, guided by their human sheepdogs.

We followed the last group on foot to a neighboring farm where we'd been invited for a *réttir* party. It turned out to be the horseback-riding family's farm. The wife was none other than our Heidi Klum lookalike. We traipsed up a muddy driveway, past the farmhouse, and toward the barn.

An overwhelming smell of urine hit us the moment we stepped inside. Not just a gentle unpleasantness but a putrid, full-on stench of stagnant urine. This was, after all, a barn.

The inside had been swept and tidied for us, boards placed between the tops of empty pens to form makeshift tables. A buffet had been set out: cheeses, lamb pâté, a few kinds of salads, some cheerfully frosted cakes, all clearly homemade. We were starving.

At the end of the buffet, a woman handed us each a small paper cup into which she ladled some of the famous Icelandic meat soup. The bright yellow broth held a few diced carrots and a small wad of lamb on the bottom. I sniffed it, but all I could smell was the barn.

Timidness overtook us. There wasn't much mingling of the groups. We mostly stood in our various social clumps, sipping our soups, waving gnats off our slices of cake. Behind me, a gray-haired woman swayed back and forth on a folding plastic chair while playing haunting tunes on the accordion.

Outside, the light was just beginning to dim. The smell, though still noxious, wasn't quite as bad anymore. I'd grown enchanted with the ancient ritual of it all, the remote otherworldliness of where I was and what I was experiencing. At which moment pretend-Heidi's teenage son skulked past me, iPhone in hand, metal music screeching from his earbuds.

On the way back to our hostel, Reynir turned off the main road and up the hill back toward our morning's horse farm. Just beyond it was a quiet mineral pool adjacent to the town elementary school. Ragga had arranged for it to stay open, and we had the place all to ourselves.

One by one, we filed through a side door and into a small room. The door closed behind me and my eyes adjusted to the dim light. I glanced around and realized what had just happened. I was trapped. The moment I had feared and dreaded was now upon us.

The only way out was to get naked.

When I'd first heard about this part of the agenda, I yelled an emphatic, "Oh hell *no!*" and threatened to pull out of the trip entirely. My friend Cirilia, a wisp of an Audrey Hepburn, had tried to reassure me that while it was indeed awkward, it wasn't *that* bad. Of course it wouldn't be for her. But I come from a long line of profoundly private people. I don't even like undressing for my doctor.

Iceland's pools are fed from the abundant, mineral-rich, geothermal springs. To keep the water clean without contaminating it with too much chlorine, they have devised a system whereby everybody must scrub-a-dub-dub all orifices before getting into the pools. Bigger facilities have a paid monitor who stands there, all day long, watching the proceedings and issuing a warning if you haven't sudsed up sufficiently. (Just think about *that* the next time you want to complain about your own job.)

This being a tiny pool, there was no such monitor, nor did we even have a chart (as the bigger pools in Reykjavík apparently did) illustrating the specific areas of concern that we were to scrub. But we were still to strip naked, line up at the two showerheads on the other end of the room, squeeze the soap dispenser once or twice, and scrub. Only then would we be allowed to put our bathing suits back on and head to the pool.

There were no stalls, curtains, or cubbies in this room. It was a cinderblock rectangle with nothing but hooks on the walls and sagging wooden benches along three sides. There was nowhere to hide.

Everyone else had taken vaguely protected spots along the wall. With a heavy sigh of capitulation, I put my things down right in the middle of the room and did it. Starting with my shoes, then socks, upward I went, until I had removed every piece of clothing from my body. I even took off my glasses, hoping that my own blindness would magically extend to everyone else. I stripped buck naked in front of women—friends, students, fans, admirers—who had paid for the Clara Parkes Iceland Experience. Boy were they getting it.

We all stepped carefully lest we bump into someone, and wouldn't *that* be awkward. It was hard to know where to look. I glanced to one side just in time to get a full-on display of boobage. I overcorrected by looking to my left, where, oh dear, a woman was bending over. I yanked my head back to center and just looked straight ahead, trying not to. . . . Wait, was that a bruise or a tattoo I spotted? If only I hadn't taken off my glasses.

Emboldened by my act (or eager to get it over with), I led the pack to the shower and pressed the red button. A fine mist of lukewarm water sprayed from high above. I squirted and sudsed, flapped my arms and legs to make it perfectly clear what I'd scrubbed, and then I stepped aside for the next person. Who, with the rest of the line, was standing right there pretending she hadn't watched what I'd just done.

The only thing less graceful than stripping in front of a room full of women is putting on a bathing suit when you're sopping wet. I fumbled and stumbled and nearly fell facefirst into some particularly bountiful cleavage before finally managing to yank everything up and tie the straps. This was my karmic revenge for what I'd done to those sheep today. I'd been grabbed, tagged, and sorted. Having lost my final shred of pride, I headed for the pool.

Which was, as it turned out, well worth the humiliation. We steeped in steaming water, heated from the depths of the earth itself, while moody, snow-capped mountains gazed down at us. In the distance, the setting sun had turned the Snæfellsjökull glacier bright pink.

Someone had left an inflatable beach ball by the pool. Reynir (who was still grumpy from being locked out of the men's dressing room by our one resident couple) picked it up and spiked it into Fanney's face. She gasped, grabbed the ball, and retaliated. Soon we had a full-scale volley. The pool's bottom was coated in a slippery mineral muck that made moving a challenge. We mostly took turns making dramatic leaps that went exactly nowhere.

Later that evening over candlelight and glasses of wine, we compared notes on the bruises forming on our thighs—gifts from the horns of all the sheep we'd wrangled. Ragga pulled out a cardigan and showed us how she cuts a steek. Lou Skyped with her cat, others shuffled sweater pictures to one another from their iPads. In the next room, a TV was playing *Grease*, compete with Icelandic subtitles. We all sang along to "We Go Together," the knitters in one room, Icelanders in the other.

The next morning, we loaded up and headed north across moonlike terrain. We dodged glistening potholes and navigated bridges that got narrower and narrower until, finally, we reached one that belonged more on a miniature golf course than a formal roadway. Reynir stopped at the peak and yelled, "Everybody out for a swim!" Amidst our cries, he explained, Ragga translating, that the bridge was actually too narrow. He couldn't open the doors for us to jump out, even if he tried.

We stopped at another grocery store and partook in more yarn; donned white cotton gloves to touch centuries-old handknits at the textile museum in Blönduós; continued to consume our weight in butter; and added swans and a lone falcon to our list of wildlife sightings. Over time, the persistent dramatic beauty became almost exhausting. Darkness gave welcome relief from the constant stimulation.

We returned to Reykjavík after sunset, our headlights joining a few others in what Ragga identified as an Icelandic traffic jam. And a day later, we assembled at a long table for our farewell dinner. We'd drunk our wine, made sentimental toasts, exchanged email addresses, and crunched the caramelized tops of our crème brûlée, but Ragga had one final surprise in store for us. Outside the restaurant, a row of taxis waited to whisk us to the suburbs, to a church where Ragga has been leading a knitting group for several years. Tonight was their big autumn gathering, we were their guests, and I was their guest of honor. They'd even announced the event on the radio.

The room was barely half full when we arrived. The more outgoing members of our group immediately trotted off, inserting themselves into conversations in that endearingly loud, unselfconscious way of Americans abroad. I, on the other hand, excused myself and went to hide in the bathroom. I always get jitters before public appearances. I worry that nobody will come, and I worry that the few who *do* come will be colossally disappointed.

When I did emerge, the room was full of women. Gone were the supermodels in high-heeled boots, the Viking reenactors in Converse sneakers. These people were quieter and more real. It looked like my old knitting group back home. Needles were already in motion, the room a murmur.

Following Ragga's command of "Go mingle!" I took a deep breath and picked a nearby table. I walked up, put my hand on one of the empty chairs, and asked, "May I sit here?"

They glanced at one another, confused. Finally, their ringleader, a prison matron in a black leather blazer, looked at me and shook her head. I rebounded to the next table where they, too, consulted one another and shook their collective heads.

I spotted Helen from Rhode Island, perched at another table. She was knitting away while the others ignored her. She looked up at me and smiled a defiant smile that said, "I'm going to sit here *all night* if that's what it takes."

It was all going so terribly wrong. This evening was to be our cross-cultural triumph. Armed with nothing but the universal language of knitting, we would break down our cultural barriers, hold hands and sing "Kumbaya." Instead, it seemed like we'd blundered into something that wasn't ours. I returned to Ragga's table to lick my wounds.

Door prizes were another revelation. In the United States, the giving out of door prizes at any knitting event is like a game show. Everyone hollers and applauds for the prizes and winners. But here, as Ragga pulled names and handed out prizes (mostly copies of her knitting DVD), I soon realized we were the only ones making any noise. Everyone else seemed mortified at being singled out when their name was called. We quieted down and prayed we wouldn't be picked.

When I finally got up and tried another circuit, I did find some people willing to talk. I met an older woman who'd knit a complete pair of mittens that night. Her granddaughter was with her, and we talked about Ravelry and popular hand-dyers and I gushed about how great it was to buy yarn in supermarkets here. She patently explained that this wasn't actually considered a universally good thing. The availability of cheap yarn in the grocery stores hurts the smaller, more selective yarn stores. Just like it does in the United States.

Later that night I remembered the blanket I'd hoped to knit out of my supermarket yarn. It had already been reduced from a throw to a lap rectangle, the bouncy Icelandic roads telling my stomach I needed to keep the rows short and my gaze on the horizon. Now, I was determined to finish it—regardless of what *it* ended up being. I would not bring home yet another unfinished project to add to my pile of unfinished projects. If this was to symbolize my time in Iceland, it had to be finished *in Iceland*. I became determined to pack as many stitches into that thing as I could, as many experiences and lessons learned, before binding off, slipping the keys under my apartment door, and catching the bus for the airport. I wanted my departure to be steeped in symbolism.

The church bells tolled a fifteen-minute final warning as I plowed through that bind-off row. I'd been holding two strands together to make it go faster, but I'd still barely made a dent in the yarn. What would I do with all the leftovers? The Skyr was gone, and I'd poured the last of my Mjölk down the drain. But here, I faced a conundrum. My bags were already bursting with several sweaters' worth of Plötulopi. I could only fit the lap rectangle or the leftover yarn. Not both.

Ragga had left for a gig in the States, and I was too embarrassed to ditch my yarn on her doorstep. After a quick hunt, I unzipped one of the couch cushions and tucked the yarn inside. I had just enough time to grab my bags and run for the bus. But I like to think that a little bit of me remains in that apartment, waiting for the next knitter to arrive.

When you first touch Icelandic wool, you might think it feels itchy, even off-putting. And so the Icelandic people, too, seem to have their soft and prickly parts: what they show to outsiders and what they reveal to one another.

In Iceland, you take the scratch with the soft, the darkness with the light. It's a place of contrasts. Of many sheep and few words, of haunting vistas and freshly upheaved earth, of methane-powered garbage trucks and family trees spanning a thousand years. Pick a town, and half the people will be related, most will have seen each other naked at the local pool at least once.

It's a lot to absorb. But with time and a good, long soak, it seeps in and leaves you longing for more.

BIG FLEECE AND FRIED
DOUGH: West Friendship, Maryland

AFTER THE LONG MAINE WINTER, it's always a shock to arrive
in Maryland that first weekend in May. The air is so warm and sweet, the
trees in full leaf, the dogwoods already past their prime. I fly through Dulles,
an inconvenient airport but an essential part of the ritual. It makes me think
of Madame Gehrels, my AP art history teacher, who first introduced me to
this architectural landmark in high school. More than that, it reminds me of
my grandparents, who lived nearby and begrudged this monstrosity when
it was first plunked smack dab in the middle of nowhere in 1962. And last
but not least, Dulles affords me a nice long drive north toward Frederick and
then east, through an increasingly rural landscape, to the Howard County
Fairgrounds and the Maryland Sheep and Wool Festival.

Though some might be older, few fiber festivals are as legendary as
the Maryland show. It was launched in 1973 as a one-day Sheep and Wool
Crafts Festival in Carroll County, attracting just 1,500 visitors. It soon
became a two-day event, and by 1980 it had outgrown its home and was
moved to the Howard County Fairgrounds in West Friendship, just a half-
hour west of Baltimore.

Entry has always been free, with funding provided by the Maryland
Sheep Breeders Association, and with additional support from the state
agricultural fair board. That will be your first and biggest clue that this
event, despite its overarching retail side, is deeply rooted in the agricultural
tradition. Whether in the show ring or the adjacent barns, the sheep are
the real beauty of Maryland Sheep and Wool. More than 600 of them are in
residence all weekend. You get to watch young people caring for sheep, or
showing their sheep, listening intently to the judges, proudly pinning their
hard-won ribbons to the back pockets of their jeans. People come to take
shepherding workshops, to watch shearing demonstrations, to find out

about the latest, greatest livestock techniques. This is where the culture of sheep and wool, in its essence, is celebrated and passed on from one generation to the next.

The fairgrounds are buzzing with setup on Friday, with sheep and merchandise alike being unloaded from vans and trailers. A few civilians will wander about on their way to one of the more than forty shepherding or fiber arts workshops that began on Wednesday and run through Saturday. People come early to learn about everything from hand-carding and needle-felting to basic shepherding and methods for determining if your sheep need deworming.

While the gates are never locked, the fair doesn't officially open until Saturday morning. At the crack of dawn, two sets of uniforms appear along the sleepy two-lane road outside: cops and Boy Scouts. The festival has grown so big in recent years that Howard County police officers show up in full regalia to direct traffic. At the height of the Saturday morning festival crush, traffic backs up nearly two miles to the closest freeway exit.

Once off that main road, the Boy Scouts take over with their freshly pressed uniforms, waving their orange hazard flags and looking adorably earnest if not slightly overwhelmed. Their task is to convince tens of thousands of drivers to park in orderly lines within a vast field that was only mowed a few days earlier. A good hour before the event begins, cars are already streaming in, people headed toward the gates, the air thick with the smell of lamb meat over flames.

In addition to the farmers showing their sheep, more than 250 vendors are set up across six barns and four exhibition halls, spilling out into fields and parking lots. Most vendors sell yarn, fiber, textiles books, tools, and even dye plants, but not all the vendors are directly related to sheep or wool. There's the man in overalls who's been cheerfully making and selling brooms for years. Or the couple that specializes in old hotel silver. Or the creepy guy hawking hunting knives. Who gets in, and how the volunteer-led committee decides this, is shrouded in mystery.

One thing is certain: Once you've managed to get a booth at Maryland, you don't give it up. It's like a rent-controlled co-op on New York's

Upper West Side. You include it in your estate plans. "He left a wife," the obituary could read, "two sons, two grandchildren, and one booth space in the Main Exhibition Hall at Maryland Sheep and Wool."

Eager beavers have already slipped in and surveyed the merchandise, browsing the booths and occasionally nudging vendors to sell before they should. Like sands on a beach, the vendor lines shift slightly each year. When I first started going, The Fold had a line easily 100 people deep. A decade later, Miss Babs and Jennie the Potter are both completely picked-over by 10:00 AM. Always, there's a line outside the 4H barn for T-shirts and other festival souvenirs—and, always, another line outside the women's restrooms. The lines seem to feed on themselves. We spot a line and get in it before checking to see what it is. Can so many people be wrong? Nowhere is the human flocking instinct more obvious than at a sheep-and-wool festival—and, in particular, Maryland.

Over the PA system, a steady soundtrack of announcements plays. It's been the same man all these years, his deadpan delivery never changing. He scolds the owner of a blue Ford Taurus, Maryland license plate repeated three times, for leaving a dog inside the vehicle. "If you do not return to your vehicle *immediately*"—he pronounces each syllable of that last word slowly—"the Howard County Police will have no choice but to liberate the animal by any means necessary." The next minute, it's a report of a lost child. You'd be surprised how many upstanding parents lose their children on these fairgrounds. Other times, it's a lost husband, or news of a sheepdog trial that's about to begin. Always, the same voice, low and slow, shifting from cheerful to fierce as events warrant.

Those who stood in line with armloads of yarn for an hour, two hours, emerge from the checkout line triumphant. "What'd you get?" is the greeting. "I snagged three skeins of Zombie Grandma," says one person, to which the other responds by showing a skein of something called "Skanky Hag" in the exclusive Formica Puppy colorway. (Hand-dyers are like microbreweries when it comes to naming things. The more nonsensical, the better.)

Pictures are posted on the Internet. Stories are circulated. Who has the biggest line? Who is the It vendor this year? Grand projects are plotted, excuses made, schemes hatched, sweater quantities stuffed into bulging bags.

Soon we run out of arms to hold all our purchases and the walks of shame begin. I use *walks*, plural, intentionally, for nearly anyone on his or her first trip to Maryland will make more than one walk back to the car. We smile and nod at one another in the parking lot, that unspoken, "You too, huh?" of the mutually guilty.

Back on the fairgrounds, the pace soon slows to a collective saunter. It becomes impossible to get anywhere quickly. Entering barns is like being swallowed by an earthworm. It's best to surrender to the natural flow of its digestive tract, knowing, eventually, you'll be pushed out the other side.

Feet begin to operate independently of the head. Our eyes dart to and fro, overwhelmed yet still trying to take it all in, while our feet, not quite receiving the signal to stop, keep propelling us forward, barn by barn. We're like kids in a moving car, swiveling our heads behind us rather than breaking our gaze. We walk into one another. Baby strollers make the terrain even more perilous (another reason to wear closed-toe shoes).

Meanwhile, our natural signals of hunger become jammed by the sight of other people eating, by the smell of food cooking all around us. By 11:00 AM, we're suddenly famished and ready to spend an hour in line for lunch.

Nowhere does the notion of "reasonable eating" go further out the window than at the Maryland Sheep and Wool Festival. You'd better like lamb because that's all you'll find. Lamb sausages, lamb kebabs, lamb gyros, lamb chili and stew. If there's flesh on the menu, it came from a sheep. The only exception being the food vendor in the permanent food building, who gets away with selling your basic mystery meats in tube and patty form.

Maryland is the place where freeze-dried scallions count as a vegetable, where I tasted my first deep-fried Twinkie, and where a bucket of glistening french fries slathered in Velveeta passes, quite reasonably, for lunch. Need a snack? Help yourself to a bag of candied nuts from the guy stationed outside the main barn. Do not be dismayed if your cone of vanilla soft-serve "ice cream" retains its shape long after melting. Or maybe you'd like a funnel cake? This fried dough squirted with strawberry goo and sprinkled with powdered sugar is a major festival tradition. Just be sure to eat it *before* the fat has time to coagulate. What happens at Maryland stays at Maryland, except for the food, which will remain in your arteries forever.

Last year, one brave newcomer managed to slip in with fresh tamales—including, *gasp*, vegetarian ones with shiitake mushrooms and kale. You could get lime-marinated coleslaw on the side. No mayonnaise in the slaw, just vegetables. Word spread like wildfire. Business was swift. The line grew. And just as we were adjusting our ideas of what to expect at the festival from now on, organizers caught wind of change and shut it down. The vendor was told to leave that vegetarian garbage at home. This was a sheep-and-wool festival and they were to sell lamb tamales only, no exceptions. We'll see if they're allowed back.

Tables are at a premium at mealtime, as are benches. Soon people sprawl wherever there's shade. Like pigeons, we line up under the eaves of barns. We gather in shade spots under trees. Some years, the heat is unbearable—once it topped ninety degrees. Packed cheek to jowl in a barn filled with wool, it's easy to wonder if you've lost your mind. But other years, a glorious, temperate wind keeps the flags waving.

By the afternoon, the crowds and starch and sugar begin to take their toll on even the strongest of constitutions. We become artificially stupid, unable to think clearly or make wise decisions. Vendors love this time of day. The rest of the lines shift over to ice cream, or soda, or Styrofoam cups of instant coffee, anything offering the sugar or caffeine we mistakenly think will give us more energy.

When the stupor strikes, I head over to the animals for relief. Here is where I can see and touch wool on the hoof. Not just one or two sample breeds, but usually forty in total, representing the full spectrum from puffy white finewools to curly ringleted longwools and dual-coated primitives alike. Their bleating noises become your entertainment, the high-pitched urgency of a lamb or the deep, guttural belch of a Romney ram. One by one, we all begin imitating them.

The sheep are there to be shown, judged, and sold. They tend to be overheated and nervous but otherwise oblivious to the human politics of the event, unimpressed by the number of skeins you bought or the blue-ribbon Corriedale fleece you managed to snag at the fleece show and sale. Your regret over that last tub of curly fries goes completely unnoticed. All of which makes the barns a great place to be.

The more gregarious sheep will approach any outstretched fingers, sniffing to see if they hold any treats. Sometimes they'll even lean against the gate so you can scratch their cheeks. You connect with others who've come for the same solace. Visiting the sheep barns restores one's faith and sense of order in the world.

As you amble in the quieter barns, your eyes are better able to appreciate what your fellow festival-goers are wearing. Gatherings such as Maryland give us a rare, much-needed opportunity to show off our work to peers who appreciate it. The only challenge is climate. This being Maryland in May, wearing a knitted sweater is foolishness. Those who don't knit light tops of cotton or linen will choose, instead, to adorn their shoulders with a shawl or shawlette. Some of the most extraordinary lace I've ever spotted has been at the Maryland Sheep and Wool Festival.

Inside the fairgrounds, any knitted item is fair game for conversation. A tap on a shoulder, an "Excuse me, which shawl is that?" will inevitably lead to a friendly chat with a stranger. Contact beyond the fairgrounds is a little more risky. I once scared a woman at a nearby Mexican restaurant when I touched her sleeve and said, "That's O-Wool Balance! My favorite yarn!"

Maryland is a long way to travel from Maine for just two days. That's a lot of money to spend on an event that changes very little from year to year. Yet I always do. My grandparents had lived in Maryland, just over the Potomac from DC. Theirs was that tiny mythical house hidden by forest, encircled on all sides by development. After they died, it was swiftly bulldozed to become part of a $4 billion waterfront resort and mini-city. We were all heartbroken. It left me feeling as if I had unfinished business in the region, and this festival gives me a reason to keep coming back. Each time I do, I greet a few more ghosts and go away a little more clear, more settled.

Just as the festival has helped me grapple with my ghosts, it has accumulated plenty of its own. By the 2000s, Howard County police were managing crowds of more than 70,000 people. With such a huge influx, it was only a matter of time before things started happening—which they did in 2008.

The Knitter's Book of Yarn had just come out and I had the great idea to bring a project from the book and let the yarn vendor who'd supplied the yarn display it in her booth. It was the Optic Waves shawl, a masterpiece of hand-dyed orange and yellow mohair. The stitch was simple feather and fan, but the yarn gave it the heft and warmth of a sleeping Maine Coon.

Just a few minutes after the show opened on Saturday morning, I heard the announcer's voice over the PA system. "If anyone has found an orange shawl, an *orange shawl,* will you please return it to the Brooks Farm Yarn booth? I repeat, an orange shawl . . ." My gut fell. Not two minutes after it had been hung up in the booth, someone slipped it off its hanger and carried it away.

Later that night, hundreds of dollars worth of merchandise would be stolen from several vendor booths in the main building and the nearby barns. Cash registers would be pried open, and all the goat pens and rabbit doors opened. Thankfully all the animals were safe and recaptured on Sunday morning, but the spell was broken. Since then, police have become a significant presence at the fairgrounds.

I'd wanted to think that knitters were different, that our gatherings were somehow sacred and safe. But the unfortunate truth is that we are not. In that way, Maryland has helped me grow up. It's been the doorjamb on which I mark my own progress. I came to my first Maryland not knowing a soul, making more trips back to the car than I care to admit. I ate my meals alone and stayed at a seedy motel in Columbia, slipping my credit card to the clerk through a slot in bulletproof glass.

Then, in 2003, *Knitter's Review* readers began to gather on Saturday at lunchtime right outside the main gates. We put faces to online names. We made virtual friendships real. We met spouses and significant others, Sherpas brought along to help carry goods to the cars. We taunted one another with our fibery finds, taking turns saying, "Wait, where did you find that?!"

We came from all over. Shelia from New York, now living in Oregon. Jennifer from Virginia. Martha from Philadelphia. Beth, who seems to have lived in a different place every year. And me from Maine. Maryland has become that annual spring gathering we do not miss. It's a touchpoint, that class reunion we attend—even if we have nothing new to say—to honor our friendships and keep track of the passage of time, all in a place that reflects a mutual love of wool.

And the festival? What began as a showcase for educating people about sheep and sheep products remains exactly that, powered entirely by volunteers, only on a much larger scale. A good amount of what formed the heart of those early shows—the wool sale, the spinning and weaving demonstrations, the barbecued lamb, and even the crowning of a Lamb and Wool Queen—continues today.

Perhaps the best thing about Maryland Sheep and Wool is that it takes place over not one but two days. Those who come for just one day must squeeze it all in, the hysteria, the ambling, the stupor. But spread over two days, it becomes something else entirely—a deep, quiet, and enduring rite of spring.

LUCKY IN LOVELAND:
An Interweave Summons

MENTION THE NAME LOVELAND to anyone in the fiber arts, at least anyone who was around between 1975 to 2014, and they'll likely say one thing: Interweave. For nearly thirty years, this otherwise innocuous little town on the eastern slopes of the Colorado Rockies was home to one of the most influential publishers in the textiles world: Interweave Press.

As the story goes, in 1975, a young Linda Ligon quit her day job as a high school English teacher to stay home and take care of her three children. From her kitchen table, backed by $1,500 from her teacher's pension, she launched a brand-new publication for handweavers. It was the perfect marriage of her two passions, weaving and words.

Linda sent her first issue of *Interweave* to friends, family, regional guild members, weaving businesses that were just starting up at that time, and anyone she thought would be interested. When people started sending her money and the subscription requests started coming in, she knew her dream stood a chance. With relentless persistence, she built *Interweave* into a quarterly magazine that's now known as *Handwoven*. Four years later came *Spin-Off*, then *The Herb Companion*, *Interweave Knits*, and *Beadwork*, not to mention hundreds of books.

Linda's success hinged on one particular truth: The narrower your subject niche, the more passionate and loyal your readership will be. She often used that passion as a currency for obtaining content, creating contests to generate feature stories for the magazines. The currency extended in-house, too, where staff was often expected to take on additional projects for the love of the craft alone—like when she convinced Deborah Robson to edit the new *Spin-Off* magazine on top of her full workload as a book editor for the company. Such was Linda's draw, and the draw of the environment she'd created, that people rarely said no.

Having long since outgrown her kitchen table, Linda had moved the offices to a stuccoed, late-Victorian home at 306 Washington Avenue, just up from Loveland's tiny old downtown. There the company grew, staff ever-expanding, until she purchased the historic First National Bank building on Fourth Street, old Loveland's main drag, in 1990. Even that proved too small, and they soon expanded across the street and next door, adding satellite offices in New York, Boston, and Philadelphia.

By the time she sold Interweave to Aspire Media in 2005, the company had seventy employees and was worth an estimated fourteen million dollars.

Soon after that acquisition, I was invited to Loveland by then-president and publisher Marilyn Murphy. Her invitation was simple: How'd I like to come for a visit? They'd pay my way and put me up. What did I think?

For a knitter, a summons to Loveland was like an aspiring country musician being invited to Memphis. It meant big things were afoot. I suspected this was it. I was about to take a journey that would result in a press release, a big announcement. They wanted to buy *Knitter's Review* for an untold sum that would set me up for life. They would hire me to stay on in some amazing editorial capacity that meant even more money, exotic travel, and free Post-Its for life. To preserve the "wow" impact of that press release, I told nobody of my trip.

I flew into Denver well past dark, rented a car, and drove the fifty-one miles due north to Loveland. Linda's husband had since walled off the downstairs of that original stuccoed Victorian building for his own use. The upstairs was converted into an apartment for Interweave visitors. On that first night, I would have it all to myself.

The building was dark when I arrived. Retrieving the key from under the front doormat gave me goose bumps. I was holding the key to the original Interweave building in my hand, walking up stairs trodden by Interweave's first editors, into rooms in which Interweave's first staff had worked. It smelled of mildew, but it was Interweave mildew, and all I could think, as I put away my belongings in one of the two guest bedrooms, was *how romantic*.

The next morning I awoke early and donned the one vaguely office-appropriate jacket I still owned, with a Knit Happens T-shirt underneath for good measure. I downed a cup of milkless tea that tasted faintly of mildew and set out.

The house was on a residential block of humble older homes, most built in the early 1900s. I passed tidy trees and lawns and picket fences, then turned left onto Fourth Street and walked the several blocks into Loveland's old downtown, a charming museum of 1930s main-street architecture. Wide sidewalks and flat-fronted brick facades were occasionally interrupted by a slick 1960s plate-glass windowed storefront with a "For Rent" sign in the window. "This is it," I kept thinking. This was the moment I would replay in my mind again and again, the story I'd retell to my great-grandnieces and grandnephews when they asked where the family fortune came from.

Soon I was there, standing in front of the old First National Bank building. Built in 1928, its white Classic Revival facade looked impressive and permanent, like how you'd want to draw a bank in a children's book.

I opened the doors and walked inside.

"I'm here to see Marilyn Murphy," I said to the woman at the desk, feeling both terrified and emboldened by being there to see such an important person.

I gazed up at the balconied second floor, which wrapped around me on all sides. I saw cubicles, desks, people. *Interweave people.*

Sure, to the less enlightened, it may have looked like any other office setting. But this one held staff whose publications I understood and revered. To me, every single person I saw that day was the luckiest person in the world for getting to work there.

Tall, elegant Marilyn appeared, dressed in the kind of creaseless artisanal perfection you'd expect from the president of a textile-themed publishing company. Around her neck draped a perfectly folded, richly textured scarf—spindle-spun, dyed with twigs and bark, and woven on a backstrap loom, I presumed, by some remote Peruvian artisans. I immediately broke into a sweat. We shook hands, spoke a few words, and ascended the central staircase together.

She led me into her office, which, at that moment, seemed fabulously grand and presidential. Looking back, I can't remember much about it except that it had some of the only windows facing onto Fourth Street. Then we went into Clay Hall's office next door, recently vacated (if my memory serves) by Linda. Here was the new owner of Interweave, a Bozeman, Montana–based twenty-five-year publishing veteran who specialized in acquiring and growing what he called "enthusiast titles."

In my mind, his office was sparse but even more presidential, with chairs positioned to make his desk seem as big and impressive as possible. The office décor may have included a fish or a sailboat, those being Clay's main interests. He was quick to point out that he'd been taught how to knit after the acquisition. It made good PR, though I doubt he ever did anything beyond a garter-stitch square before tossing it away and getting back to his deals.

Up first was a meeting with the *Interweave Knits* staff, which had been assembled in a room for the sole purpose of meeting me. Marilyn introduced us and left. We made awkward small talk at first, nobody quite certain what the goal of the meeting was. I asked about the acquisition and they opened up. People in the company were optimistic but nervous about how it would pan out. Apparently, Clay had been very clear with everyone right up front: His was a five-year plan to fatten the calf and sell it onward and upward. Which meant more opportunities, but also more projects, more magazines, more work. Somehow, "do it for the love of the craft" didn't have the same ring when it came from someone backed by private-equity firms. The profit focus had become a little too obvious.

When the meeting adjourned, Ann Budd offered to clear my mug for me. At that time, Ann was the managing editor of *Interweave Knits* and had already authored some of the most dog-eared books in my knitting library. You can't have *the* Ann Budd clearing your dirty dishes, and I said as much to her. I insisted on taking it down the hall and into a side kitchen. She walked with me, then pointed and said, "Shove it there." She gave a wry smile, "Now you can tell your readers *the* Ann Budd told you where to shove it."

Soon it was lunchtime. Clay, Linda, and I headed across the street to exactly the kind of casual upscale restaurant you'd expect as the setting for a very important business meeting. They sat on one side of the crisp white-clothed table, I sat on the other side. *This is it*, I thought. This was when they would pop the question and name their number, which I would consider, oh so sagely, before accepting.

While Clay wolfed a panini and Linda effortlessly made a bowl of soup disappear, I ordered a salad that took about nine months to chew. We made more small talk. Clay told me all about his new sailboat. He had a jovial demeanor and spoke with a slow, old-boy Southern drawl. Linda's eyes never left me, her mouth fixed in a tight-lipped smile that made me increasingly nervous. She was friendly and smart but impossible to read.

We went back to the bank, met up with Marilyn, and headed into a bigger meeting room where Ann, Linda, and others had gathered. This time, they wanted to talk books. Like a kid being invited to the North Pole to pick out her Christmas presents, I fired out idea after idea. I started with my biggest dream of all, to write a whole big beautiful book all about yarn.

"We already did that," Linda said, pointing to a three-ring binder on the bookshelf behind me. It was a book about yarn for weavers. It hadn't done very well. "What else do you have for us?"

"I think there's a market for a book about creative spaces, where I profile inspiring, successful people in our industry and showcase the space where they create. Like, Linda, that wooden kitchen table where you founded Interweave."

She looked at me. "I think we slaughtered a pig on that table...."

"Or you, Ann?"

"It'd have to be the shower wall," she replied. "I do all my best thinking in the shower."

By the sixth or so idea, Linda interrupted, "Where do you get all these ideas? Do they just come to you?" Her smile remained as inscrutable as at lunch. I couldn't tell if she was impressed or just being polite. Was she secretly plotting to break into the apartment tonight and chop me up into little bits?

By the end of the meeting it was somehow decided that my first book with them should be a small black-and-white paperback about the curse of the "love sweater." It would feature a collection of personal stories from famous knitters either proving or disproving the age-old superstition that knitting for a loved one before you're married will curse the relationship. Because every knitting book must include patterns, this book would also feature charming teddy-bear sweaters, each designed by the famous knitters telling their stories. To be honest, this wasn't really my first, or second, or even third choice for a book. But still, it looked as if my lifelong dream of writing a book was finally going to come true. We would firm up the details when I got home.

I floated back to the apartment on a cloud, exhausted and elated from what had just happened. And it wasn't over, either. That night I would dine with the president of Interweave, and surely that's when she'd pop whatever question had caused them to invite me to Loveland, and I would accept. Tomorrow I would fly home, triumphant. In anticipation of the celebration, I called up my airline and cashed in 20,000 frequent-flyer miles for an upgrade. It seemed only fitting to fly home in first class with all the other successful businesspeople, what with everything coming together so smoothly.

That evening we went to another slick restaurant on Fourth Street. We drank a Malbec wine that turned Marilyn's teeth an inky shade of blue. My salmon "on a plank" consisted of a piece of salmon on a cedar shingle exactly like the ones we were using to reshingle the back of our farmhouse. I was still so nervous that I sat on my hands, and when I pulled them away from the vinyl banquette they made a loud fart noise I hoped Marilyn didn't hear.

As we talked, it finally dawned on me that Marilyn had been steadily pushing Loveland as a great place to live. Pushing as if any future between Interweave and me would hinge on my being closer. I'd just left San Francisco, very decisively, to pursue a quieter, more creative life in Maine. I'd managed to carve out a job for myself in the knitting industry that was fulfilling, autonomous, and self-supporting. As I stared at my cedar plank, I was left with a simple, heartbreaking certainty: This train would need to keep going without me.

The fish sat heavy in my gut that night. Sometime during the wee hours, I awoke with a start. I thought I'd heard a man's scream. Was it outside? I heard nothing else, no running footsteps, no wailing, no sirens, nothing. Heart pounding, I turned on the fluorescent overhead light and was startled by moths, dozens of them, fluttering around the ceiling. I heard a clock ticking in the other room, and a slow, steady drip from the bathroom shower.

Marilyn picked me up the next morning for a final breakfast before I left. She took a detour to show me Lake Loveland. By now, she'd learned that I loved to sail.

"See?" she pointed at the bathtub-toy sailboats floating in the shallow water, "You can sail here, too."

But by then I think we both knew it wouldn't work out. Like strangers on a first date, we'd reached that critical moment when one person reveals a love of cheese, the other, incurable lactose intolerance.

We said goodbye and I headed for home. As sad as I was that there would be no press release, no big announcement, I knew I'd made the right decision. And I still had a book deal. For a paperback about sweaters people knit for their boyfriends and girlfriends. Featuring teddy bears. But that was still something, right?

I returned home to my routine and I waited.

The call came almost three weeks later. It was from someone else, someone whose name I didn't recognize. She'd been out of the office the day I came, she explained. But she understood I had an idea for a book? Yes, I said, and laid it out for her. That's very interesting, she said, not sounding interested at all. She suggested I write up a proposal and send it to her for consideration. Things were pretty busy right now, but she'd take a look and get back to me in a few weeks. She briefly explained how to write a book proposal, she wished me the best of luck, and we hung up.

Not only was there no press release, no offer of any kind, but if I wanted this odd little book (that I already knew I didn't want), I'd have to fight for it. And I was now out 20,000 frequent-flyer miles.

One week later and entirely out of the blue, I got a call from an editor who was launching a new knitting imprint at Random House. Had I ever thought about writing a book? she asked. By the end of that phone call, from my very own kitchen table, I'd struck a two-book deal with an option on a third. The first book would be my beloved ode to yarn, *The Knitter's Book of Yarn.*

Clay's company would eventually go on to be acquired by an even bigger fish, F+W Media. Linda's still there, but Clay cashed out to "do some fishing and bird hunting and let opportunity find me," he told *Folio.* In the spring of 2014, the bank building was shuttered and all 130 employees were moved to an anonymous office park in Fort Collins.

But in my heart of hearts, Interweave will always be that grand old bank on Fourth Street where I first got to sit at the big kids' table and where *the* Ann Budd told me where to shove it.

GLASS, GRASS, AND THE POWER OF PLACE: Tacoma, Washington

THE MADRONA TREE is a marvel of the Pacific Northwest. A tall evergreen with broccoli-like foliage, its slick pumpkin-colored bark gradually peels away, like chocolate shavings, to reveal a tropical green skin underneath. The tree doesn't transplant well, and where it does thrive, it's the preferred nesting site for anything with wings. In short, it's a beautiful, rare, and popular place to call home—as is the Madrona Fiber Arts Winter Retreat, which has been happening every February in Tacoma, Washington, since 1999.

Knitting retreats tend to be similar from place to place. You have workshops, a marketplace, evening social activities, and, through it all, you have ample space to spread out, make yourself at home, and hopefully form meaningful connections with other knitters. The flesh of nearly every fiber-related gathering hangs on such a skeleton.

What, then, makes one event different from the next? In the case of Madrona, it begins with place. The four-day event is held inside a museum of American art glass loosely disguised as the Hotel Murano. It's not just a pretend museum to lure tourists to the hotel, but a real showcase with curated exhibits of more than forty-five renowned artists. In the main lobby, it's hard not to gawk at the stunning Chihuly piece suspended from the ceiling. Functionally a chandelier, it has snakelike glass arms that curl outward into delicate tips. When the light hits it just so, the silver glass takes on a warm, golden glow.

Every floor of the hotel displays the work of a different artist, with photos and stories that also influence the guestroom decor. Each room key has a different picture of a featured art piece, along with the floor number where you can find it. Mine would have an intricate glass bustier by Susan Taylor Glasgow, fifteenth floor. Guests are encouraged to ride the elevator to the top floor and tour the collection, one floor at a time, until they're back down at the lobby.

Art glass owes much to the Pacific Northwest. American glass sculptor Dale Chihuly grew up in Tacoma, and he founded his Pilchuck Glass School here in the 1970s. Just a few blocks from the hotel is the Museum of Glass, a 75,000-square-foot showcase of art glass from around the world. It was installed along the waterfront during revitalization in the 1990s. All of this is to say that, whereas most conference-size hotels have the personality of a bowl of oatmeal, this one really does reflect the community it serves.

And then there's the organizer. Over the years, the Madrona Fiber Arts Winter Retreat has been relentlessly shaped by a nearly invisible, enigmatic yet passionate fiber artist named Suzanne Pedersen. You won't find her on Twitter or Ravelry, and she probably thinks *hashtag* is a culinary term. She is not at all eager to jump on stage and be the center of attention, yet she is fiercely focused on and protective of this event.

Suzanne does things the old-fashioned way. She writes long emails explaining the history and underlying cultural principles of Madrona. At its heart, that culture pivots on two simple ideas: learning and community. Most other retreats hope for the same, but they throw in an element of commerce and self-promotion that sometimes overshadows the rest. Madrona is not sponsored by a profit-driven corporation, by a big magazine, or by a yarn company. It is self-funded, born from the very same Pacific Northwest fiber community it serves. Today, the event draws more than 900 people each year.

An invitation from Suzanne is a clear indicator that you have, in fact, arrived. You could say that everyone who is anyone in the knitting world has taught at Madrona, from Cat Bordhi to Stephanie Pearl-McPhee, Nancy Bush, Evelyn Clark, Judith Mackenzie, Sally Melville, and Amy Herzog, a list that barely scratches the surface.

My invitation came in 2013, after I'd been writing and teaching for more than a decade. Suzanne and I had emailed back and forth for years. We'd even met at Sock Summit, where she snuck into one of my lectures

and then sat me down for an informal interview afterward. It seemed like a
lot of work for a teaching gig, but I was flattered and eagerly accepted.

Tacoma sits on Commencement Bay in Puget Sound, about forty
minutes south of Seattle. The port city gained notoriety in 1940 when its
brand-new suspension bridge, nicknamed Galloping Gertie, twisted so
violently in heavy winds that it collapsed just six months after it opened,
prompting the study of aeroelastic flutter.

I left a Maine that was buried deep in February snow, landing on a
persistently gray, but snowless, other side of the continent. While waiting
for my shuttle, a group of Emirates flight attendants clicked by me in their
pumps. Their tailored tan blazers and flared skirts were a welcome contrast
to the flannel pajama pants I'd been seeing all day, worn by travelers who
have no qualms about rolling out of bed, grabbing their pillows, and head-
ing straight to the airport. But these women had signature red pillbox hats
perched atop cowl-like white gauze veils that draped across their chests like
a string of pearls. We all stopped to admire their procession.

It was dark by the time my shuttle van pulled into the hotel. Exhausted
from a day of travel, I probably would've grabbed a granola bar and hit the
sack early were it not for the fact that I'd shared a ride—and commentary
about those Emirates flight attendants' uniforms—with Catherine Lowe and
her husband.

Catherine is a quiet lion in the knitting industry, someone who keeps
a low profile while upholding the highest standards in everything she
does. Her couture knitting workshops span days rather than hours, requir-
ing students to commit to her and her alone for the duration of any major
event. And the workshops always fill up. She has taught at Madrona for
years. Where most patterns occupy six or eight pages, hers can span thirty
or more for a single garment. I remember Catherine proudly telling me
that she'd managed to shorten one pattern . . . down to eighteen pages.

She and her husband live in a farmhouse in upstate New York, equi-
distant from Boston and New York. In her previous life, she got her PhD in
French from Yale (with a minor in Italian) and was a college professor for
many years. Her husband was the head of the Columbia University library

system before taking over the Boston College library. He wears a silk cravat, grows peonies, and is an amateur jeweler.

You know how some people aren't big talkers at dinner? Or they talk *too* much, barely pausing to notice what they're shoving in their mouths? Catherine and her husband are neither of those things. They are charming and eloquent, well traveled, well read, and well spoken. They know their wines and have a fine appreciation for the art of the table. When they invite you out for dinner, no matter how long a day you've had or how far you've flown, you don't even pause for breath before saying yes. And so I did, enjoying far too many courses and far too many wines whose names I couldn't pronounce, hitting the sheets at an hour my body thought was 4:00 AM.

I awoke a few hours later. While the event wouldn't officially begin until the next day, the hotel was already crawling with knitters. Just sneaking out of the hotel for groceries took nearly an hour, I met so many old friends and acquaintances on the way. If I was going to see anything of Tacoma before work began, develop any kind of cultural bearings that would help me connect with local students, I needed to plan an escape—and fast.

I hopped a bus uphill toward Martin Luther King Jr. Way, where my iPhone told me good Vietnamese pho could be had. This brothy noodle soup has always been my go-to cure for that groggy first day in a new place.

A two-dollar bus fare and a mile uphill later I was in a quiet neighborhood of little businesses and somewhat shaggy-looking apartment buildings. I found my restaurant and took a table by the window. Soon my pho came, I squirted the requisite Sriracha and fresh lime, tore the cilantro leaves, dropped in the jalapeño and bean sprouts, and gave it a stir.

Just as with touch, flavor has a way of bringing the world into focus. The stronger and more potently soothing the taste, the more familiar and reassuring the associations, the deeper and clearer that focus becomes. I sipped, and sipped, and sipped, with each spoonful of broth pulling me back together. A good wool has the same restorative powers.

Sated, I wandered back out to explore the neighborhood. I passed the Johnson Candy Company, which looked like it hadn't changed much in fifty years. Ditto the hospital uniform store next door. Just beyond that, a cheerful mural depicted a streetcar chugging by a busy farmers' market, red and white awnings flapping in an imaginary breeze. There was no such market, streetcar, or breeze today, just clouds and threat of rain. I strolled past a vast medical complex, the air humming with ventilation systems and a sense of urgency.

I reached a grungy coffee shop that claimed to offer Tacoma's finest—complete with a disapproving barista with excessive facial hair. I took my cup into a park I'd noticed across the street, gulping its contents before reaching my next destination: the beautiful and historic W.W. Seymour Botanical Conservatory. Inside, a riot of color greeted me, blooming tulips, azaleas, impatiens, and daffodils. Walking farther, the greenery changed to ferns, clivia, orchids, bougainvillea, low palm trees, Spanish moss, and weird clusters of alien-looking plants in little wooden boxes suspended from the ceiling. I found a bench tucked in a corner, with a green stone dragon peering over my shoulder, and pulled out my knitting. The air smelled lush and sweet.

I don't know why exactly, but whenever I knit in public, people take it as a sign that I want to be interrupted—perhaps even saved from what they might perceive as a terribly tedious task? A steady stream of onlookers wandered over and wanted to talk. "Oh look, honey, she's knitting," a husband nudged his wife. "Now that looks comfortable," said another man. "See, now, I can't do that," apologized a woman.

I was in PR mode. I showed them what I was knitting and explained that it was made from the downy undercoat of the Arctic musk ox. I let them touch the fiber and I smiled as I watched their expressions soften in pleasure and surprise.

Having chatted with my quota of non-knitters for the day, I tucked my knitting into my bag and left. It was time to walk back toward town and begin Madrona in earnest. But I got distracted by an odd building on my left. It looked like a cross between a post office and an old Masonic temple, but with a pair of pretend Greek temples stuck on either side. Spotting a blue-and-white plastic OPEN sign stuck to the front door, I went inside.

A lone man was working and rushed over to welcome me. It was a
private museum, he explained. The founders, California real-estate moguls
David and Marsha Karpeles, had amassed the world's largest private
collection of original manuscripts and documents. This was one of twelve
museums they'd established throughout the country.

We have this and this and this, he told me, rattling off names faster
than I could register them. He kept running off and returning with more
things for me to see, all photocopies. The rescue report for the *Titanic*.
("We also have a model of the *Titanic*, it's over here, if you'll follow me ...")
President Nixon's letter of resignation, signed with a ballpoint pen. The
August 6, 1945, flight log from the *Enola Gay*. "See that?" he pointed to a
notation on the log. "That's where he dropped the bomb."

My guide became more and more mysterious as we went along, allud-
ing to things in the collection that were far too important, too confidential,
ever to be displayed. Eyes narrowing, he whispered, "Some very important
people don't want you to see things." Then he straightened up and asked
loudly, "So, what brings you to Tacoma?"

Back outside, I gave up on waiting for the bus and headed downtown
on foot. The road leveled out and offered a clear panoramic view of the
waterfront. Steam from the factories mingled with passing clouds. I saw
the massive robotlike cranes of the Port of Tacoma and the striking outline
of Mount Rainier in the distance.

From here, I walked back downhill toward the Theater District and
my hotel. The bars had a restive frontier-town vibe, the marquee at the
Old Pantages 1917 vaudeville theater advertising "Sweet and Spicy: A
Valentine's Day Burlesque." The illuminated windows of LeRoy Jewelers—
proudly serving greater Tacoma since 1941—looked cozy and inviting.

As I got closer to the hotel, I saw more shawls, more smiling faces
that greeted me by name. Knitters were arriving en masse now. Cars were
double-parked alongside airport shuttles, valets helping unload suitcases,
carry-on bags, tote bags, grocery bags, and spinning wheels. While many
came from within driving distance, others had flown in just for the show.
Inside, the lobby was now chockablock with knitters, sprawled on every

sittable surface, clustered on couches and armchairs and coffee tables. They were checking into their rooms, they were at the bar, they were headed up the glass stairs and over to the elevators. Everyone was smiling, hugging, exclaiming, and petting one another's handknits. This Brigadoon manifestation of the Pacific Northwest fiber elite had officially begun.

A hand-drawn welcome sign, propped on an easel, was the only indicator of what was to come. At the registration desk upstairs, the scope of the event was laid out as clear as day in manila envelopes—each representing one happy person—stacked upright in plastic bins spread across table after table after table.

The next few days unfolded as these events do, with early wake-ups and full classes of bright, engaged people having a glorious time. Mealtimes were a marathon for teachers and students alike, as hundreds of us descended upon the hotel's restaurants, needing to be seated, served, and checked out in ninety minutes. Questions abounded. "Is the gravy on the poutine vegetarian?" "Will the Thai noodles take long?" And, of course, "Should we all just split the bill?"

During the few off-hours, I made a quick perusal of the market, watching more knitters and spinners fall even deeper down the rabbit hole. Some three dozen vendors filled the room, each hand-plucked by Suzanne. I found mainstream, hand-dyed, and breed-specific yarns galore, as well as all sorts of needles and tools, bags, buttons, spinning fiber, mugs, and even soaps. While many large events charge admission to their marketplace, or limit it to paid attendees, it is a point of community pride for Suzanne that this marketplace is free and open to everyone.

Although the three-hour and six-hour and two-day classes had filled months ago, several dozen shorter mini classes were still being offered to late arrivals. But many clusters of friends skipped classes entirely, instead installing themselves at one of the large tables that had been set up throughout the hotel for this very purpose. People came and went, and soon each table was heaped with belongings.

On Friday and Saturday afternoon, there were book signings, too. Unlike most other big events, the Madrona staff doesn't stock and sell books as part of the signing, nor do they coordinate with any of the vendors to do so. Clever vendors will peek at the author list ahead of time and bring popular copies to sell in the marketplace, but otherwise, it's just authors at a table in the rotunda by the marketplace, making themselves available to anyone who wants to talk or get something signed. It's a low-key way to connect with readers, though it probably doesn't make publishers very happy. Because most of my books weigh over a pound each, very few people bothered to schlep them to the show. Instead, I gave my scribble to anything that was presented me. A show program, a tote bag, even an outstretched arm was fair game.

I wish I could tell you about the annual Teacher Talent Show for Charity, benefiting Doctors Without Borders, the Global Fund for Women, and Heifer International. I wish I could tell you what outlandish things we teachers agreed to do for this fine cause. But, alas, the whole evening was under strict media blackout—rules made clear many times by the evening's organizer, Stephanie Pearl-McPhee. Nobody wanted to wake up the next morning and see their embarrassment broadcast all over YouTube.

In exchange for our efforts, our songs and dances and sundry performances, the audience offered up more than $10,000 in donations. Respecting the media blackout, I will only note that my particular group performance was so bad, so painfully disharmonious, that we closed the show. Stephanie grabbed the mic and announced that she'd shut off the music for $100—at which point a woman sprinted up to the stage, bill in hand.

All this silliness was fine and good, but the very next evening, I was to be the featured banquet speaker. My topic: a heartfelt glimpse into the American textiles industry. Mustering up what dignity I had left, I took to the stage just as the carrot cake was served, and I finished the Q&A as the tables—and my still-uneaten piece of cake—were cleared away. The lobby bar would continue to do swift business until closing time.

The days were thick and demanding, during which I can't say I had any "Aha, so *this* is Madrona" epiphany. Like any good event I've attended, the spark seemed to come from what the people made of it. There were definitely clusters of friends for whom this was an annual tradition, their own personal version of Thanksgiving. But even they were still welcoming to newcomers.

I doubt most attendees had any idea how much work went on behind the scenes, the fertilizing, tilling, weeding, and tending that took place so that they could plunk themselves down and effortlessly grow. This appearance of effortlessness, perhaps that's the key.

After the last class let out and the marketplace closed on Sunday afternoon, I found myself high above the city in a hospitality suite with the other teachers. We gathered around the table, discretely trying to make the free hors d'oeuvres our dinner.

Here, Suzanne exerted her final dusting of self over the event. One by one, she beckoned us to the couch. We sat, hands politely folded in our laps. We talked. I stole glances at the clipboard in her lap, at the envelope with my name written on it and presumably containing a check. "How did it go?" she asked. "Did you enjoy yourself?" "Is there anything we can do better?" She thanked me for my work. She provided her feedback, all positive. Then she went over the numbers, tallying them up with a calculator, to make sure we both agreed on the sum of the check. I got my envelope and said thank you.

The logic of who gets asked back is often apparent only to Suzanne. She is very insistent on not repeating teachers more than a few years in a row—unless she wants to, in which case she'll have you back so often they might as well name a suite after you. The algorithm is hers alone.

I was among the lucky ones. At the end of our meeting, she popped the question and, of course, I said yes. But something made me suggest that we let a few years pass before I returned.

I wasn't ready for Madrona to become a "thing." There's a reason Brigadoon only reappears every 100 years. I wanted to preserve its magic a little while longer.

CLOUDBURST OVER PARIS

I'D PROMISED THEM no yarn stores, no fiber festivals, no chasing down that elusive sheep farm someone said *might* be in the next town. No endless waiting while I fondled, took notes and pictures, and transformed a perfectly fine family vacation into yet another business trip.

My nieces grew up having to share me with yarn. They learned early on that any time with Aunt Clara would likely mean a festival, or a mill visit, or at least one lengthy stop at a yarn store. And, always, some form of work deadline.

In 2013, Hannah had just turned seventeen and Emma was about to turn fifteen. My brother—feeling flush, or perhaps finally realizing how quickly they were growing up—had announced plans for a grand European tour that summer. Together with my mother they would visit Switzerland, Austria, Germany, and Denmark. And their first stop would be Paris.

France means a great deal to me. Play a few notes of Edith Piaf and I'm waxing nostalgic. It's where I came of age, as they say. I ordered my first beer and received my first marriage proposal there, though not at the same time. It's where I first learned about the pleasures of the table, the slowly prepared meals that take all afternoon to enjoy. I fell in love with fountain pens there, and I mastered the art of looking stern and disinterested on public transportation. After college, I fled back to France—to the city of Nantes—in the hopes that a life would reveal itself to me there. Alas, it did not.

The more fluent I became in French, the more critically judged I felt—and not just by my language, but also by my behavior, my clothing, my ideas, and even my body. My French friends only had to snicker and announce "So American" at whatever I'd just done and I'd be deflated. My roommate, Laurence, was looking through pictures of me as a child once and said, "You would be so pretty if you weren't fat." It wasn't an insult, she insisted, just a fact.

My fragile ego could only withstand a year of this before I finally gave up and ran back to the land of coddling and free hugs. I avoided France for decades, like a jilted lover. The longer I stayed away, the more those initial memories were replaced by grand and mythical ones until I'd built an impossibly beautiful time capsule of France. I wasn't sure I could ever return for fear that the reality of the place would destroy my airbrushed memories and leave me with nothing.

But when my brother told me of their plans, when I envisioned my young nieces setting foot in that magical city for the first time, I knew I had to be there. I couldn't let them stumble blindly through the tourist traps and leave thinking they'd seen the place. They agreed, and after twenty-one years of staying away, I booked myself a ticket. The promise being, let me repeat myself, that there would be no yarn stores.

I arrived a day before they did. Charles de Gaulle airport, the signage, the machines, even the *currency* of gaining access into the city, it had all changed. I figured it out just in time to help an even more lost Canadian catch the same train as me into the city. His friends were renting an apartment, he explained. He was just here for three days, then off to Amsterdam and London.

"I should be able to get a pretty good sense of Paris in three days, right?" he asked.

His name was Gerard, he worked in finance, and he wore fine, chestnut-colored Italian leather shoes.

"What do you do?" he asked.

"I'm a writer."

He raised his eyebrows and nodded, as if to say, "touché."

"I write about knitting."

Now he laughed. "Well, at least you're writing."

Eventually his stop came and I wished him a good three days. Off he went.

Switching from commuter train to Métro, my sensory memory woke up. I recognized that sweet, slightly burned tar smell in the air, the wobbly low note of warning followed by the *woosh-clang* of the car doors shutting and locking. Musicians were busking in the subway corridors, Peruvian panpipes, a violin, an electric guitar. Two young men hopped into my car as the doors were closing and started playing an upbeat tune on accordion and saxophone.

Some things had changed. Gone were the tiny newsstands that used to nest beneath the curved walls along the platforms. Instead, vending machines offered neat rows of M&Ms, potato chips, gummy bears, and Snickers bars. Since when had the French embraced snacking?

We headed west from Denfert-Rochereau, passing all my old stops like flipping through the pages of my diary. There was Montparnasse, Duroc, Falguière, and then we slipped above ground into the Parisian version of Mr. Rogers's neighborhood. The morning sun reflected off the buildings, colorful geraniums spilling from the wrought-iron balconies. I took deep breaths to calm my butterflies.

I got off at La Motte-Picquet Grenelle and glanced across the platform. There stood a dozen young men in old-timey vests and suspenders, knickers, argyle socks, and driving caps. One sported an enormous handlebar mustache, another a curved pipe. I looked around but nobody else seemed to notice or care. Since when did such a sight *not* draw the collective disapproval of everyone? I wanted to shake my fist at those youngsters, to yell, "In my day, I couldn't even wear *tennis shoes* without being laughed at!"

I deposited my bags at my hotel and immediately set out to explore the neighborhood. My niece Hannah had wanted to pick the hotel. When you're a dreamy seventeen-year-old girl from New Mexico, you naturally want to stay near the Eiffel Tower, so that's where she put us. But now that I was there, I had to admit that she'd chosen well. We were in the 7th arrondissement near rue Cler, a pedestrian market district with a neighborhood feel. Women were pushing their little market carts, elderly men slurped their coffee while gray-muzzled dogs slept at their feet. People lined up at the outdoor counter of a *boulangerie* (*pace yourself*, I cautioned). Outside a florist's stall, buckets of voluptuous pink peonies beckoned.

I kept walking past a chocolatier, a butcher, an Asian take-out. I paused at La Sablaise fish market, probably because it was everything a fish market isn't back home. Bright and clean, its walls were covered with jaunty maritime murals. Baskets were filled with crabs and mollusks and bivalves of every description. Whole fish, long and slender, short and stout, reclined on beds of brilliant white ice. None of them seemed bothered at having been caught. Another case showed off delicate, almost translucent cuts of fresh fish that smelled only of sweetness and the sea.

On I went, past a hardware store. A few doors down I started at the sight of . . . what were those, skeins of yarn? Cupping my hands on a glass door, I looked closer. It appeared to be some sort of yarn store, with pastel Phildar yarns on the tiny shelves, '80s baby sweater leaflets stacked on a nearby table. I pulled back and looked for a list of hours, a name, anything, but found none. I would check back every day but never find the place open, not that I could have gone in anyway because, let's remember, *no yarn stores.*

On my way back, I paused at a realtor's window to pick my imaginary apartment. A simple, two-room affair with windows overlooking rue Cler was currently listed for a cool 605,000 euros—at that time, just over $830,000 US. Perfect.

The rest of the day was spent speeding across Paris, opening the time capsule I'd sealed twenty-one years ago. Street by street, I replayed the favorites of my past. There it was, my old pharmacy, my old school. My apartment building still stood, prettier than ever, its facade recently cleaned, the old drafty windows replaced by energy-efficient ones. My window was open, and someone had put flowers on the balcony.

I followed a woman down my street. She was wearing exercise clothes and carrying a yoga mat. Inconceivable twenty-one years ago. I once made the mistake of leaving home in sweatpants and everyone—everyone, I tell you—turned and stared. My greengrocer was gone, the Vietnamese restaurant now Korean. It was refreshing to see that Paris hadn't kept itself in suspended animation after I'd left. If it had moved on, then I could too, right?

Early the next morning, my family arrived. We did the full tour, hitting

every item on the teenage girl's Greatest Hits list for Paris—but with a few
edits by yours truly. We took a boat down the Seine and climbed the Eiffel
Tower. We tried on shoes and dresses, licked cones of Berthillon ice cream,
rode the Ferris wheel high above the Tuileries, sighed at the Monets in the
Musée d'Orsay, and whispered to one another in church after church.

I forced them to put butter on their baguettes in the morning, and
I made sure they sipped a cool Orangina under umbrella-topped tables
in the Luxembourg gardens. We even sampled a tray of oysters at La
Coupole. Rather, I sampled, they shook their heads.

But on day six, I woke up in a funk. The city was in the grip of a heat
wave, and my tiny hotel room had no air-conditioning. (Correction: I
hadn't yet discovered that what I *thought* was a TV remote was, in fact,
the control for the in-wall cooling unit.) The idea of a full day of touristing
en masse left me a little queasy. I told my family I'd sit this one out. They
headed off to Sacre-Cœur without me, and we agreed to meet that evening
on the Île Saint-Louis for dinner.

Only it wasn't just the heat that had gotten to me. I'd been overcome
with an accumulation of emotional jetlag, a collision of past and present
that left me not quite sure where or who I was. After five days of flipping
through the pages of a very old diary, I needed something to pull me into
the present.

Over my café crème on a busy boulevard near rue Cler, aided by free
Wi-Fi and a thing called Facebook, I was tapped on the shoulder by a
ghost from the past. My old roommate Laurence was now living in Paris.
She'd seen my pictures on Facebook. Was I really in Paris? Could I join her
for coffee?

Just a little while later, I stepped off the Métro at Charonne, walked
a few steps to the Le Rouge Limé, and hugged a vision from the past who
was, in fact, both very real and very familiar.

There in the flesh was the same face, the same big head of curly hair,
the same perfect teeth and beautiful laugh. We had not seen or spoken to
one another in two decades. Babies had been born and grown to adults in
that time, cell phones had been invented, the Internet had taken over.

Yet at that moment, time folded into nothing. We took turns pointing out each line on each other's face, each gray hair, and none of it hurt my feelings now. I was too surprised at how fundamentally unchanged she was, how unchanged our friendship. We'd been close. Then life happened and somehow we lost touch. Occasional emails had been lobbed back and forth just to be sure each person was still there.

She told me about her daughters and about what it's like to be a single woman in Paris. Internet dating is alive and well, but, she complained, "Once you hit forty, the only guys who approach you are in their eighties."

I told her about my move to Maine and she told me about her grandmother's old home on the coast. She and her brothers had pooled their savings and bought the place. They all go there every August. "It's magic," she said. "The door is always open. Everyone comes and goes. We all eat together in the garden. You'll have to come." I told her about my own magical farmhouse on the coast, how the door is always open, how everyone comes and goes, and how she, too, would have to come.

The trip had been a leap of faith. I was trusting that the present wouldn't destroy all those memories that I'd held so dear. I'd spent the week flying through the air on an emotional trapeze, and hugging Laurence goodbye felt like letting go. I needed someone, something, to catch me on the other side of *now*. And I knew exactly what that something was.

A few hours remained until I was to rejoin my family. I turned on my phone and used up the last megabyte of my data plan to look up a yarn store. If I hurried, I could make it, and my family would never know.

Now, Paris has several places where you can buy yarn. The most famous is probably La Droguerie. This is an old-school French yarn store, the kind where you're expected to know what you want when you walk in, where endless fondling is discouraged. There are no couches where you can linger for a few hours and chat with friends. Try to take a picture in La Droguerie and you'll be *tut-tutted*.

The other traditional option would be the yarn department at Le Bon Marché Rive Gauche. But I needed more than a respectable display of brand-name yarns in a department store. I'd heard about a newcomer, a softer petting zoo of a shop that combined yarn and tea. For months already, I'd been stalking its owner, Aimée Osbourn-Gille, on Instagram. Her pictures were always warm and cozy and inspiring.

After two Métro transfers, I was in a neighborhood I'd never visited before. Tucked in the 13th arrondissement, Butte-aux-Cailles sits squarely between Place d'Italie and rue de Tolbiac. This area of Paris is best known for its large immigrant population—"large" by French standards means, as of 1999, some 24 percent of the residents. A particularly sizable number of those immigrants come from former French Indochina, which may be why the 13th is also home to Paris's Chinatown. The Pitié-Salpêtrière teaching hospital is here, once the largest hospital in the world, built atop the former dumping grounds for prostitutes and madwomen, aside the maze of tracks leading to the Gare D'Austerlitz.

In the 1960s, entire blocks of the 13th were sacrificed to the urban renewal that added the first skyscrapers to the Paris skyline. Today, the area is being carved up yet again, this time to make way for the shiny, slick glass facades of a brand-new Paris Rive Gauche neighborhood.

Despite the encroaching gentrification, Butte-aux-Cailles remains a neighborhood of real people, of Parisians going about their daily lives, walking their dogs, hanging out laundry, playing with their kids. Sounds from a television drift through an open window. You can actually find a parking spot. If you're like me, you'll find yourself entertaining two parallel thoughts: *I could live here* and *I could probably even* afford *to live here.*

Huffing and puffing up a particularly steep hill and winding around a few sharp corners, I finally came upon a colorful sliver of a building with my destination at its tip: L'Oisive Thé, which translates loosely as "the idle tea." Its tall windows were open, and people were seated at tables on the sidewalk.

What had seemed enormous in my imagination was, in fact, a wee bird's nest of a place jammed with mismatched tables and chairs, cozy lamps, and knitting books heaped on shelves and windowsills. Along the walls, I spotted a rainbow of familiar faces: Koigu, Madelinetosh, Lorna's Laces, Juno Fibre Arts, Old Maiden Aunt, Shibui. These were yarns I knew well, from people I also knew well—not twenty-one years ago, but now.

As I stood there taking it all in, Aimée herself walked through the front door carrying a tray of dishes from an outside table.

She tilted her head to one side and asked if I was, in fact, who she thought I was. We dismissed an awkward handshake for a hug, then an offer of water, or tea, a spot to sit. Would I like to join that evening's knit-in? The knitters would arrive any minute. Was I sure I didn't want some tea?

By the kitchen, an open basket suspended from the ceiling held apples, oranges, and a single bruised banana. Bulk tea was lined up in cheerful canisters painted bright yellow, with Fauvist flowers and leaves that matched the sign out front. The names of the contents of each canister, too, were painted in beautiful cursive. *Assam. Camomille. Menthe.*

The more I looked, the more I noticed. Children's drawings had been lovingly taped along the wooden wainscoting below the kitchen bar. Each table, each chair, even each tablecloth was different, sporting flowers, polka dots, abstract swirls and zigzags, in shades of pink, orange, red, yellow, blue, and gray. Taken together, it felt as warm and velvety as the inside of a peach.

L'Oisive Thé would be a remarkable shop no matter where it was, whether in Paris or even Kansas. Which, as it turns out, is where Aimée is originally from. She, too, had come to Paris as a college student. She'd met a boy, Gilles, and had fallen in love. He tried to join her back home in Kansas, but as the song goes, *How ya gonna keep 'em down on the farm after they've seen Paree?*

Gilles suggested they return to Paris, and her family encouraged it. As a young woman, Aimée's mother had made the journey from Korea to join her husband in the States, and she knew both the hardship and possibilities of such a big move.

Aimée took the leap and off they went. They married in 2002 and had two children. Back in Kansas, Aimée had enjoyed a successful career managing marketing for the industrial equipment manufacturer Caterpillar Inc. But once in France, she discovered that her degrees and experience were essentially useless. She would have to start over from scratch.

By 2008, she and Gilles were looking around at all their friends buying houses and starting families. "We looked at our lives, and it came down to this," she told me. "We could buy an apartment and be in debt for twenty years or more, or we could take out a loan and start a business I'd been dreaming about for years—and be on our feet again within seven years." They chose the latter.

Entrepreneurism hadn't really taken hold in France when I lived there last. Starting up one's own company, going freelance, not only were these foreign notions to most French, but they also went against the very culture of the place. Young people were supposed to know what they wanted to do by their early teens and direct their studies toward that goal. They'd get a *stage*, followed by a job that they would likely keep until retirement. The system was just beginning to break down when I left. Students were emerging from school to find no *stages*, no jobs. They'd done as they were told, but the system couldn't keep its end of the bargain. The same thing was happening in the United States.

As its name suggests, L'Oisive Thé was originally conceived as a tearoom. A skilled baker and a tea connoisseur, Aimée was also an avid knitter, so she dedicated a small space in her tearoom to hand-dyed yarns from England and the States. These were yarns nobody had ever seen in France before. At first, she said, it was a hard sell. "People were used to paying twenty-five euros per kilo, and here I was asking that much for one skein?"

But with a lot of sacrifice and hard work, she has cultivated a loyal and appreciative customer base. That single shelf soon became a wall, which has since taken over most of the shop. You could say she has been a key figure in bringing France's knitting culture into the twenty-first century, with not only hand-dyed yarns but also knitalongs and Stephen West workshops. She is now living the dream, one that includes plans for expansion, and it suits her.

One by one, the members of her TricoThé knitting group arrived. We made introductions. They were chatty and enthusiastic. Just back from Norway, one woman quickly pulled out a skein she'd bought on her trip. We *ooh*ed and *aah*ed and discussed all the things she could make with it. Ours was the same conversation I've had with knitters everywhere.

I couldn't help but wonder how different my life would've been if this shop, this community, had existed in Paris twenty-one years ago. Maybe I would've found myself and stayed after all? No, I had to leave in order to find my way. But to return and find community for who I am now, it gave me a deeply calm, settled feeling. I'd caught the other swing of the trapeze.

I didn't have any knitting on me, a problem Aimée was more than happy to remedy. But yarn in my bag would have been lipstick on the collar to my family, proof that I'd broken my promise, that there *had* been yarn stores on this trip.

The women were lovely and the chairs so inviting. How I wanted to stay and hear more stories, but family beckoned, and I was resolved to keep what remained of my promise to them.

A summer downpour began as we were saying our goodbyes. Aimée handed me an old-fashioned clear hoop umbrella that someone had left behind. It felt fitting to move through the streets in a plastic bubble, still observing without quite being back *in* it. As my Métro car passed over the Seine, the clouds parted. Rays of sunshine hit the choppy waters and reflected back in a million tiny sparkles.

That evening, my family and I enjoyed dinner at a guilty-pleasure tourist trap that even the locals enjoy at least once. We piled onto long benches at communal tables and ate "as they did centuries ago," yanking vegetables from a basket for our salads, cutting slabs of pâté, eating meat on skewers, and filling pitchers with wine from a large wooden barrel. A gray-haired man came by with his guitar and sang folk songs to us. Everyone joined in, whooping and cheering and stomping their feet. Long-forgotten lyrics spilled out of my mouth.

Tomorrow, we would part. I'd fly home, and my family would board a train for Switzerland. Ours would not be a sad parting, as I knew I'd see them again soon. And my parting from Paris would not be sad either, for I knew I'd see it again soon—and the next time, there *would* be yarn.

A THING FOR SOCKS AND A VERY BIG PLAN: Portland, Oregon

THE CITY OF PORTLAND, OREGON, has long enjoyed a reputation for the quirky. The home of Voodoo Doughnut and Powell's Books, the inspiration for the hit TV show *Portlandia*, a birthplace of food-truck culture, and host to the Velveteria: Museum of Velvet Paintings *and* the World Naked Bike Ride, Portland has never been one to reject the unusual. And so it was that, when a pair of knitters approached the Oregon Convention Center about renting it for a sock-knitting conference, little debate ensued over what the answer would be.

The Sock Summit was the offshoot of "seven lunatic women with a thing for socks and a very big plan." At its heart were author and blogger Stephanie Pearl-McPhee (better known as the Yarn Harlot) and hand-dyer Tina Newton, aided by a dedicated staff of volunteers.

Along with Debbie Stoller, Stephanie shares the distinction of being one of the only knitting authors to hit the *New York Times* bestseller list. Hers has been the Oprah of blogs, with one mention holding the potential to make or break upstart designers and yarn companies. By the sheer force of her personality alone, she managed to raise more than $1 million for Doctors Without Borders. She does not do things small.

Which is why nobody was actually surprised when the news came out that she and Tina had rented out the Oregon Convention Center and were planning to stage an event there. Were we pleased and excited? Yes. Surprised? Not really.

This was 2009. Ravelry had been live for just two years and was still in beta. Major knitting conferences were still the domain of the XRX/Stitches franchise, with Interweave's Spin-Off Autumn Retreat maxing out at just 200 people. Only after the runaway success of this show did Interweave and the publishers of *Vogue Knitting* wake up, sniff the air, and venture into the big ring themselves. It was almost inconceivable for a couple of indie upstarts to plan anything of convention-center magnitude. The fact that they intended to focus exclusively on socks seemed even crazier. But the name was pure genius: It would be called the Sock Summit.

We teachers believed in the idea, and forty of us heeded the call. It was an impressive list, with names like Nancy Bush, Cat Bordhi, Meg Swansen, Anna Zilboorg, Sivia Harding, Judith MacKenzie, Cookie A, and Anne Hanson, to name just a few. We all shared collective goose bumps upon hearing that Stephanie had managed to locate the legendary Barbara G. Walker and to lure her out of knitting retirement for what was her first appearance in decades. Priscilla Gibson-Roberts, by then in seriously poor health, was equally wooed.

Classes were scheduled on anything that could possibly relate to socks, from heels and toes to cast-ons and bind-offs, textured colorwork, arch shaping, photographing our work, and even the proper ergonomics of sock knitting. While an outsider might assume they would be hard-pressed to come up with seventy-eight sock-themed workshops that first year, in fact, the organizers had to reject far more proposals than they could accept.

I modified my Yarn 101 workshop to focus exclusively on the needs of sock knitters. It felt a little contrived at the time (I really just wanted to be there, socks or no socks), but the preparatory research was so compelling that it ended up inspiring my third book, *The Knitter's Book of Socks*. Other teachers, not all necessarily fans of the sock genre, were so eager to be a part of this pathbreaking event that they, too, gladly reshuffled their offerings.

That first year, the knitting public had been whipped into a frenzy by the time registration finally opened. Every blogger and publication and yarn store and knitting guild had been percolating news. At the designated hour and minute and *second* of registration, more than 30,000 concurrent users hit the website and scrambled for classes.

Nobody had believed the organizers when they said this system needed to be able to handle major traffic. Who could expect that from a mere knitting event? With a gentle pat on the head, Stephanie and Tina had been sent on their way, glasses of water in their hands, and reassured all would be fine. It was an experience they had repeatedly during the planning and execution of this event. By the time the second Sock Summit rolled around in 2011, they had invested in a world-class system that would, at last, work without fail.

But in the case of that first registration, all was not fine. The system quickly went haywire under the weight of so many users. Classes appeared sold out when in fact they weren't, shopping carts were suddenly emptied, error messages flashed, knitters were left bitterly disappointed.

That alone, the feeding frenzy, the ephemeral nature of registration, the luck of getting in, the randomness of having your hopes dashed by the software, created a kind of star zeal we'd never seen in a knitting event before. When the dust cleared that first year, some 1,800 people managed to snag spots in 78 classes. At the second Sock Summit, that number ballooned to 130 classes and 6,000 attendees, roughly the population of Harvard, Massachusetts. They even succeeded in getting the mayor of Portland to declare it Sock Knitting Week. As I said, Stephanie doesn't do small.

Normally at larger events, the key personality stays above the fray, relying on staff to handle the minutiae of the show. But at the Sock Summit, Stephanie was both key worker bee and star. She also taught several workshops. Staff wore earpieces and carried radios in their pockets, and more than once I watched as Stephanie was forced to interrupt a heartfelt confession from an admirer to tap her ear and start another conversation. Everyone wanted a chance to interact with her.

A few months before the first Sock Summit, after all the classes and the schedule had been set, word got out that a group of knitters in Australia just set a world record for the most number of people knitting simultaneously (at 256 people). It wasn't hard to do the math and figure out that our 1,800 registered attendees could easily blow that number out of the water—and so it was decided that we would also set aside fifteen minutes to break a Guinness World Record.

We dutifully assembled in the largest ballroom and took our seats. Having been prepped and pumped by Stephanie, we all knit for fifteen minutes without stopping. Official observers set the tally at 935 people. We were filmed and left confident that we were victorious. Which we were, until Australia's knitters fought back and regained their title. In 2011, a group in Taiwan seized the lead, and, last I heard, it was snapped up by the National Federation of Women's Institutes in the United Kingdom, which managed to wrangle a whopping 3,083 knitters for the task.

As much as I'd like to think people came to Sock Summit primarily for the teachers and workshops and for the chance to help set a Guinness World Record, the marketplace was another real draw of the show. More than 150 vendors had been assembled from across the United States and as far away as Australia.

Sock knitting was at its height. Because socks use just a single skein of yarn, sometimes two depending on the yardage, they're the perfect way to use up those hard-to-repeat skeins from independent hand-dyers. Think about it: A dyer who manages to fit six skeins at a time in her microwave doesn't have to worry about maintaining consistent colorways for larger projects if she focuses on serving sock knitters. It was a marriage made in heaven.

We had the brightest, best examples of indie hand-dyers on hand, as well as makers of tools, bags, accessories, and even shoes. It was like walking through a life-size, three-dimensional version of Etsy. What a thrill to see this vast exhibition hall, the kind usually reserved for boat and RV shows, filled instead with yarn and knitters. Members of the Teamsters Union guided semitrucks into the loading docks and unloaded cartons and cartons of yarn.

The excitement on that first opening morning was so great, the line to get into the marketplace so long, that Stephanie and Tina guarded the doors and got everyone to sing "Ninety-nine Skeins of Yarn on the Wall" to keep the masses from revolting. As soon as the doors opened, the scrum began.

The flip side of showcasing smaller producers? Smaller quantities. Like the Beatles on their 1965 world tour, vendor booths were swarmed. Shelves were picked bare within minutes of opening. It was the registration frenzy all over again, this time with the embarrassment of full, public display. Skeins were grabbed out of hands, tossed over heads, held in triumphant "neener-neener I got it and you didn't" poses in pictures for social media. Market scores became people's badges of honor. If you didn't get a skein of Goth Socks (which was picked clean by fellow vendors before the show even opened), you weren't a cool kid. Or so some wanted it to seem.

But the real gem of the show was hidden deeper in the marketplace. Past the screaming crowds and their wads of cash sat an actual sock museum with painstakingly curated examples of historically significant sock replicas from "the dawn of time" to today. We had World War II Red Cross socks, argyle socks, socks knit by Barbara G. Walker and Elizabeth Zimmermann. We had beautifully knit examples of medieval socks, Anasazi socks, and popular sock designs like Monkey, Rivendell, and Pomatomus. Walker, rather surprised by the adulation she was receiving from all these knitters, did swift business selling her old handknitted socks out of her suitcase that weekend.

At the second Sock Summit, Stephanie and Tina announced their intention to bring livestock onto the show floor. It took quite a bit of haggling with the convention center, but they won out. In the end, three sheep, fittingly named Heel Flap, Instep, and Gusset, took up residence in cozy pens near the back of the hall.

They were the stars of the Fleece to Foot contest. Six teams competed to card, spin, ply, and knit two pairs of socks out of Heel Flap, Instep, and Gusset's freshly shorn wool. I was tasked with spinning the "standard" yarn by which the teams would base their own efforts. At the sound of the word *Go!* the teams toiled until exactly 3:30 PM, when the needles were stopped. While nobody actually succeeded in finishing the challenge, a team called World Wide Mash-Up completed the most knitting and was declared winner.

We made no attempt to set another Guinness World Record at that second Sock Summit. We learned and laughed and connected; we acquired; and we even danced at a 1980s-themed sock hop. The sock hop was just a warm-up for what happened next.

Late on Saturday afternoon, I walked out into the public square in front of the convention center. Several others were already there. More knitters streamed into the square until we numbered in the hundreds, all casually milling, all with a skein of yarn in our hands.

When the clock struck 5:15 PM, the first notes of "(I've Had) The Time of My Life" from the film *Dirty Dancing* began to play over discretely placed loudspeakers. The crowd came together, everyone faced the same direction, and we began a choreographed dance in which we serenaded the skein we were holding. It may have lacked the element of surprise, and the dance may not have been visible to more than a handful of passersby, but we rejoiced in being part of the very first knitting flash mob. For those of us there at that moment, we really were having the time of our lives.

With two sold-out shows under their belt and a state-of-the-art registration system now in place, it was pretty much assumed that Stephanie and Tina would continue to ascend higher and higher Sock Summits. Even before the second show was done, people were already announcing their plans to return in another two years. Hotels were picked, roommates chosen, classes discussed before anything had been inked or announced. Then, in April 2013, Stephanie announced that the Sock Summit was no more.

Naturally, there was disappointment. Oh, how we'd looked forward to seeing what new records we'd be asked to help set, what new heights Stephanie and crew would manage to reach this time. But I suspect they were just following the cardinal rule of high-altitude mountaineering: Always preserve enough energy for the descent. "It's a round trip," mountaineering legend Ed Viesturs once wrote. "Getting to the top is optional. Getting down is mandatory."

MIGHTY SCOOPS AND PHO TO GO: Celebrating TNNA in Columbus

BOOKSELLERS HAVE BOOKEXPO AMERICA, the gift industry has NY NOW, and in the knitting world, industry folk converge twice a year for TNNA, our largest and only trade show, sponsored by the National NeedleArts Association.

Here, the people who make our world go 'round—the manufacturers, distributors, designers, agents, and retailers, to name a few—come together to network, take classes, and conduct business for the coming season. TNNA is where trends are launched, competitors are eyed, and closely held secrets are revealed. Are we headed toward novelty yarn again? You'll get your answer at TNNA. Is the pompom back in style? A quick walk through the show floor and you'll know.

As with any such trade organization or show, TNNA has strict membership requirements designed to keep out the spies, the amateurs, the kids desperate for an early peek at what Santa has in his workshop. Depending on the membership level you seek, from Affiliate to Student, Retail, or Wholesale, you may even have to share bank statements and letters of recommendation from other members. Every few years, you have to do it all again. Even the sitting president had to get two letters of recommendation to requalify when her time came.

As a yarn critic, I go to TNNA to survey the landscape, to see yarns, and to meet with colleagues. Others go because they own yarn stores, operate mills or yarn companies, publish magazines or patterns or books, manufacture needles or accessories, teach workshops—and that's just within the knitting group. TNNA also encompasses needlepoint, spinning, weaving, counted thread, and embroidery. But at a very high level, the groups break down into two worlds: knitting and needlepoint, the Sharks and the Jets of needle arts.

Despite the fact that both crafts use yarn, they've never mixed well. When a knitter gets onto the show floor and mistakenly veers into one of the stark, canvas-lined needlepoint aisles (for they are segregated), a distinct chill comes on, a sense of having left one's village and entered a strange forest. I'm confident the needlepointers feel the same when they stray from their tribe into ours.

TNNA is a volunteer-governed, non-profit trade association that was founded in 1975. It has no headquarters, no full-time staff. Day-to-day management duties have been farmed out to a professional association management company that also services the International Window Cleaning Association, the Ohio Forestry Association, and Professional Lighting and Sign Management Companies of America, among others. TNNA does offer other professional programs throughout the year, including youth mentoring, charity outreach, and industry research. But its work really comes into focus during its biannual trade show.

The main attraction of TNNA is the marketplace, where more than 250 vendors exhibit and take wholesale orders for their wares. Most vendors have one or two booths the size of what you'd expect a trade-show booth to be, while the bigger players can occupy entire blocks of rows and aisles. Décor likewise varies from the uninspired skirted table or two to slick, completely custom-built spaces with racks and shelves, upholstered armchairs, charming bicycles, and potted plants. Placement of vendors is a source of endless debate, which hand-dyer got plunked uncomfortably close to her competitor, which vendor was exiled to a Siberian end row bordering, gasp, *needlepoint*. In theory, there's a protocol to everything, but people still whisper.

Education is another key part of the show. Workshops begin a couple of days before the marketplace opens and end as the last crate is hammered shut and loaded back on the truck. Classes run the gamut from business development to social media, and always include several craft-specific topics too, like working stranded intarsia or stitching your very own needlepoint canvas depicting a Hollywood Gold Digger "all dressed up in her tight gold lamé capris ready to spend her sugar daddy's money." (Really.) Many teachers use the classes as a way to offset their TNNA travel and hotel expenses, though the pay scale is modest.

Cash-and-carry transactions are strictly forbidden except for one night, when many of the exhibitors set up in a big ballroom and sell special goodies and kits for the event called Sample It. No minimum orders, no waiting, this is pure and immediate retail pleasure. For vendors, it's a chance to get products into the hands of potential wholesale customers. For attendees, it's a chance to buy nifty stuff. They line up by the hundreds for hours ahead of time, sprawled on the convention center floor like teens trying to score tickets to a Taylor Swift concert. The doors open and in they race, treating themselves to a little of this, a little of that, perhaps a knitting bag, a shawl kit, a cute accessory, all that with no major commitment—*and* they get to carry their goodies home right then and there. (Even after an "Immediate Delivery" option was added to the show in 2015, Sample It was more packed than ever.)

TNNA has a summer and a winter show. The winter show—where summer yarns are unveiled—takes place in January, swinging generally between San Diego and Long Beach, California, with an occasional pit stop in Phoenix. While summer yarns aren't historically as exciting, the winter TNNA still gets decent traffic for the simple reason that it takes place on the sunny West Coast in January.

But the summer show—where fall and winter goods are previewed—is another matter entirely. The first summer TNNA I attended was years ago in Indianapolis. I mostly remember air-conditioned walkways and $12 convention-center hotdogs. But the next summer, we moved to Columbus, and everything about TNNA changed.

Despite occupying more than 1.7 million square feet, the Greater Columbus Convention Center manages to defy convention-center odds by fitting right into the Short North neighborhood in which it sits. Even more important than the convention center itself is what stands across the street from it: North Market.

First established in 1876, the market now occupies a huge structure built in 1995. An open retail space on the ground floor is ringed by a second-floor gallery of tables for eating. More picnic tables sit outside, though it's often too hot for them by the time we get there. Vendors sell beautifully stacked fresh fruit and produce, pungent spices, breads still warm from the oven, exquisite cheeses, all sorts of fish and meat, flavorful Indian food, mounds of pad thai, and perfect pierogies. More important than all those foods combined, though, is the ice cream. Specifically, Jeni's Ice Cream.

Back in 1996, when gourmet ice cream consisted of Häagen-Dazs, when the rest of the world was squeezing frozen yogurt out of spigots, Jeni Britton Bauer began serving up surprising flavors inspired by fresh local ingredients. I know you hear those words all the time, but these flavors are so good, so unusual, so surprising, that many of us gasp when we sample them—or moan, or laugh, or all of the above. Everyone around understands. And there *are always* people around, for there is always a line at Jeni's. It's a happy line, everyone mentally clapping their hands together as they get closer and closer to the ice cream case.

Part of Jeni's magic is the staff, who seem genuinely passionate about ice cream and dedicated to making their customers happy. I'll never forget the time the guy behind the counter heard me mumble, "I wish I could just have what I had yesterday," and responded, "Let's see, that was the lemon-blueberry yogurt with berries and whipped cream, right?"

Tasting is a key part of the adventure, and you're encouraged to sample everything. They'll patiently dole out little spoonfuls as many times as you want, whether you're tasting pear zinfandel, cherry lambic, queen city cayenne, salted caramel . . . the list goes on, and it changes from season to season. "You can try as many as you like!" they assure you after the third or fourth tiny spoon changes hands and they spot a look of embarrassment creeping onto your face.

"Which one was that?" a stranger may ask if you're particularly demonstrative with your swooning.

I know I'm supposed to be telling you about TNNA and I'm instead prattling on about ice cream, but there's a reason. This market, and this ice cream in particular, has galvanized the show. It's given us a common denominator that has nothing to do with yarn or with our business at all. During a difficult time of transition, as the once small and tightly closed industry has been disrupted by new technologies and a galaxy of new players, many of whom have bypassed the establishment altogether, and the focus of what TNNA is about has struggled to adapt to this brave new world, food has helped bring us together.

I haven't been going to TNNA as long as some people, but even I can remember when the aisles were so full it took forever just to make it from one to the next. Shop owners lined up to see new products and place hefty orders. Now, while I wouldn't say tumbleweed abounds, the crowds are sparse at best. And instead of lining up to place orders, many of those entering vendor booths are doing so in order to pitch their own services. Where have the people gone? Some no longer come, preferring to let the sales rep come to them. Others have simply stepped across the street.

North Market has provided a neutral territory, beyond the convention center and hotels, in which to hold our meetings. Rather than ordering matching Caesar salads off a generic hotel menu, whispering so that the person at the next table doesn't hear, we can wander through the market and explore the food together, each picking what we love. What better way to understand someone on a basic level than by watching how they relate to food? Even rivals have a safe starting point for conversation. Lo, we both picked the same lunch spot two days in a row. Maybe we aren't such adversaries after all?

One of my favorite TNNA meals was with Eunny Jang when she was editor of *Interweave Knits* magazine. After days of polite meetings with others, we threw manners to the wind and ordered everything at the Polish stall. There were no boundaries between my Styrofoam container and hers, just one big smorgasbord to be devoured equally.

Or the time I ran into an editor with whom I'd had a very tense working relationship. She was almost eight months pregnant, uncomfortable and exhausted. She'd slipped off her shoes and was slurping a bowl of pho not unlike the one I was carrying on my tray. I was overcome with an urge to put my hand on her shoulders and tell her everything was going to be okay.

As great as the lunches are at North Market, the ice cream has always been the kicker. Hold a bowl of it and you are instantly approachable, no matter whether you're the head of a yarn company or an unknown blogger. The greeting when passing other show-goers on the street tends to be, "Which flavors did you try today?" Ravelry's Mary-Heather Browne keeps a list on her phone so she can track her progress through the menu and avoid duplication. I keep my sampling spoon handy and am not afraid to use it if I spot a friend leaving the market with a fresh bowl.

Once North Market closes for the day, the ice cream crowd simply moves a few blocks up North High Street to the actual Jeni's *store*. There we resume our line around the block, waiting for a chance to sample yet more flavors. We're all friends—line friends—by the time we get inside.

After-hours entertainment is another integral part of TNNA, especially in Columbus. Somehow the Hyatt Regency lobby has been declared the official hangout spot. People perch on every surface, the more official folks staking out high tables at the bar, the rest of us piling onto whatever couches and ottomans we can drag into ever-expanding circles. I've never stayed up long enough, but legend has it that if you do, you might catch an impromptu ukulele jam led by *Knitty* editor Amy Singer. Yarn and needles remain in constant motion all night. It's impossible to guess how much knitting has to be collectively unraveled the next morning, in the sober light of day.

But the Hyatt lobby isn't the only place for festivities. Quite often, the summer TNNA coincides with Columbus's Gay Pride celebrations, whose parade route runs along the very road that divides us from North Market. What fun to watch the parade from the air-conditioned skyway running between the convention center and the hotel across the street, to share the moment with small-town shop owners. "Well goodness gracious," I heard one say, admiring a buff shirtless man astride a gyrating burrito, "will you look at that?" Just then, a topless woman gazed up from her float and blew us a kiss.

While the show is on, it feels like the knitters have truly taken over the town. You can't walk 100 feet without running into someone you know.

TNNA, and especially TNNA in Columbus, is like a weeklong fulfillment of that dream where we've managed to secede from the rest of the world and make our own kinder, gentler, more yarn-friendly society.

Of course, this being the Midwest in June, there will also be storms. Big, dramatic ones where the sky turns a dark shade of what you keep double-checking to make sure isn't tornado green. We've had lightning strikes, flooded roads, blown transformers. The convention center has Tornado Shelter signs for a reason. One night I was on my way to dinner with Amy Singer and we turned just in time to catch North Market's red neon sign silhouetted against a sky that had suddenly turned black and furious. We were spared, but a tornado did touch down about 100 miles north of us that night.

I'll never forget the time Cat Bordhi and I spent an extra hour in the Jeni's store while the skies unloaded outside, lightning flashing, sheets of rain whipping sideways straight at the windows. Dozens of strangers, many of us knitters, were packed together like campers huddled in tents, grateful to be dry and protected. If the power went out, we had all volunteered to eat the ice cream before it had time to melt.

With such a fondness for Columbus, you can imagine the outcry when it was announced that the show would move to Washington, DC, in 2016. The way we wailed, you'd think the world was coming to an end. But life is what you make of it, and the show is what we make of it. Perhaps it wasn't Columbus that brought us together at all, but rather our mutual curiosity, a collective eagerness to move beyond the convention center and explore the world outside.

Mind you, I'm still upset that the summer show is moving. But I'm confident that no matter where it goes, we'll find a big enough Hyatt lobby and enough ice cream to keep us afloat for another year. Plus, I hear DC has a great ramen joint not too far from the convention center. . . .

ON AIR IN CLEVELAND:
Filming *Knitting Daily TV*

WHEN I WAS GROWING UP, I wanted to be an actress. I regularly appeared in every school drama production, and I set up and became president of my high school's very first drama club. But like many, I lacked the necessary spine and drive to make it happen in the real world. The notion of constant rejection was just too much. Instead, I found comfort behind words.

How ironic, then, that decades later my writing career would land me on television. When it was all said and done, I appeared on thirty-nine episodes of *Knitting Daily TV*, a program that still airs on public television stations around the country.

Before YouTube, knitters relied on just a handful of VHS videos and even fewer television programs for any kind of "live" knitting information. Although Elizabeth Zimmermann began broadcasting her own programs on Wisconsin Public Television in 1966, the notion of knitting-related television programming never really took off. When Shay Pendray began filming *Needle Arts Studio* in 1996 on Detroit Public Television, it was big news—but it was even bigger news when she sold the show to Interweave Press in 2007. The program was relaunched as *Knitting Daily TV* and, in 2012, I was invited to join the show.

Shay stayed on for the first few years, but the producer role had been handed to Interweave's head honcho, Marilyn Murphy. After my monumentally unmomentous trip to Loveland, Marilyn had actually become my friend and mentor—and it was because of her that I got tapped for the gig.

The idea was that I'd be their resident yarn expert in a five-minute segment called "Yarn Spotlight" that would run in every episode. Then-host Eunny Jang and I would sit at a table and chat about the yarns that just happened to be spread out in front of us—but with the brilliance and clarity expected when a camera is rolling and your show doesn't have the words *Real Housewives* in its title. Having written about the science, mechanics, and magic of yarn for more than a decade, I loved the idea of leaving the page and jumping into freeform conversation.

Soon Marilyn and associate producer Annie Bakken presented me with a list of the yarns I'd discuss in the first season. I learned that each episode would be grouped by a theme, such as Superb Stitch Definition or Made in America or Brushed Yarns. I quickly discovered what would become my two biggest obstacles: I could only talk about yarns that had been placed there by an advertiser (difficult for someone whose career was built on unbiased criticism) and, because this was public television, I could never mention any of them by name. Advertisers still got to say, "That's our yarn!" when their spot aired, but I could never acknowledge them on camera. All too soon, I felt like I'd switched from PBS to QVC—though I accepted the mental challenge of following the rules while staying true to my core.

A few weeks before it was time to shoot all my episodes for the season, yarn began showing up at my doorstep. I dutifully knit swatch after swatch after swatch, some in stockinette, others in colorwork or lace, cables or ribbing, so that each yarn could be shown in what I felt was its ideal knitted state.

Then came wardrobe. While everyone else wore beautiful handknits on set, Marilyn thought it would be fun if Eunny and I did the segment in lab coats. "You know," she smiled, "like you're *in the yarn lab* with Clara and Eunny?"

Interweave had just entered the knitting conference fray with its Interweave Knitting Lab conference, and event staff all wore lab coats. All we had to do was stick white labels over the black Knitting Lab logos and we were good to go. As dreadfully unflattering as they were, and as much as they trapped perspiration under the bright lights (causing the stickers to peel off), in hindsight these lab coats ended up being a godsend. While everyone else grappled with costume changes, all I needed to bring was a few jewel-toned T-shirts to wear underneath.

The show was filmed in a suburban Cleveland studio whose claim to fame was that Bob Dylan had once filmed something there. The studio was near the back of a 1970s brick building with seedy, deeply tinted windows. It looked like a cross between a porn studio and a setting for a mob hit.

Each season had thirteen episodes, all of which were filmed over the course of one week. We shot two seasons per year, one in the spring, one in the fall. Marilyn, Annie, Eunny, and I stayed at a chain hotel by the freeway, and one or two other guests would pop in and out for their spots. Marilyn played chauffeur, renting a big car and coordinating arrivals so that we could all pile in at the airport. Before we even reached the hotel, we'd make our first stop of the week: Whole Foods.

Due to an unbearably early start time and abundance of junk food at the studio, we were encouraged to stock up on our own breakfast and snack supplies. Eunny and Annie, both being tiny women who subsisted mostly on cigarettes, would get out with a bag of grapes, perhaps some almonds and a yogurt. I, on the other hand, staggered out with at least three bags containing everything but dish soap.

The next morning, long before sunrise, we'd meet in the lobby. Eunny was always the last to arrive.

"She's like the child genius," Annie joked. "She stumbles in at the last minute and then totally hits it out of the park."

Marilyn would drive us to the studio in the rental car, her knowing the way, Annie shouting directions regardless.

The first item on the agenda was makeup, administered by a friendly freelance makeup artist in a brightly lit, mirrored room by the bathrooms. She would then give our hair a quick once-over with a brush before sealing it down with a giant can of Aqua Net. Returning from makeup was like Halloween, everyone turning excitedly to see what you'd become. People assured me I looked great, but I felt like Ronald McDonald in drag.

Once your face was on, you had to be careful. No rubbing or scratching, no messing with your plasticized hair, no drinking except through a straw, and God help you if your nose started to run. It was like walking around with wet nails, only instead of nails it was your entire face. Once the makeup artist was done, she packed up her brushes and left for the day, giving each of us a little stash of powder and lipstick for emergency touch-ups.

Next came the clothes. A studio assistant had already pressed and hung our polyester lab coats, so it was just a matter of picking a shirt that matched whatever shirt Eunny would wear under her lab coat, and I was set for the day. For the rest of her shoots, Eunny came in and out, swapping one sweater for the next from a vast heap of *Interweave Knits* extras.

In keeping with theater tradition, the studio had a "greenroom" where we all waited our turn. The walls were painted an unflattering shade of yellowish neon green that made your eyes hurt. Tables were arranged around the perimeter, and we each claimed one as our temporary desk for the week, setting up laptops, notes, bags, and snacks.

Out came the trays, giant jelly sheets like bakeries use. Each segment got one tray, and I would set about assigning all my swatches and yarns and sample garments to their proper positions. I wanted my trays to overflow with samples so that I would have enough to talk about once the cameras started rolling. The worst thing that could happen was an empty table and no words to fill your time.

Marilyn patrolled behind me, fingering the swatches.

She was not prone to effusive praise or criticism, so you had to read the signals closely. "Well, this is a lovely stitch," was cause for rejoicing.

"Is this all you have for Episode 8?" Out came the needles. Occasionally she and Annie pitched in. This was definitely a team effort.

Tables along the middle of the room were heaped with boxes shipped from Interweave. They held all the garment samples, *more* samples, *more* yarns, *more* props in case we needed them. They'd been filming long enough to know that more was always safer.

Soon, Eunny's face would appear on the big TV at the far end of the room, just above the mini-fridge and plastic tubs of pretzel sticks and Twizzlers. It was a live feed from the studio next door.

Eunny was a pro. A star blogger, she'd been hired by Interweave right out of college, and the TV gig was dumped on top of her magazine-editing duties—but she took to it like a fish to water. Her voice was always steady and calm, her face smiling and assured. Unflappable, she spoke confidently and without ever muttering "um" or "uh."

As I sorted my swatches, Eunny would begin recording one of her segments in the next room. She'd go over stitch techniques or the steps of whatever garment was being featured in a knitalong for that season. Lace, modular knitting, cables, mosaic, intarsia, all were fair game.

Once the cameras began rolling, Marilyn migrated to the control room, where she'd sit with a local producer and the switcher who pieced together each segment, from camera to camera, as it was being filmed.

Soon I'd get the call that it was my turn. As a rule, we always started with the second episode, holding off on that first episode until the very end, after we were warmed up. I'd gather a tray, take a deep breath, and go in.

The studio had a red ON AIR light by the door. Inside was a huge space with concrete floors, unused props shoved to the side, cords and cables and lights galore, and several cameras atop camel-sized tripods on wheels. At the very back, in the center of it all, was a brightly lit, human-scale dollhouse of a "room," which was our set. It had wallpaper and bookshelves and baskets, and way up top, a false ceiling complete with skylights.

At this point a handsome young man would approach me and start fishing under my lab coat. He was just clipping a microphone battery pack to the back of my waist, then running the wire around and up to my chest. But it always felt like an awkward first date, with him pinning his tiny corsage of a microphone to my collar. Once you had that mic, you *really* had to be careful. Any noise you made was immediately broadcast into the earpieces of the camera crew and everyone in the control room. I need not tell you how imperative it was that you turn off your mic before going into the bathroom.

Because distances on screen appear greater than in real life, Eunny and I had to sit knee to knee, so close that I was almost in her lap. There were rules of conduct, the most important one being that I could never, ever look at the camera. She was the only person allowed to address the audience. My job was to sit in her lap, my torso angled toward her but my face pointed toward the camera I wasn't allowed to look at, and be

intelligent and succinct and charming in one take, without ever mention-
ing the actual name of the product I was discussing. Easy, right?

Resplendent in our white polyester lab coats, we'd go over the premise
of that episode. The theme is halo, I'd tell her, and these are the yarns I had
to work with. This one (I'd point to the purple sample) has angora, this one
(pointing to the green) is all about the qualities of mohair. I'd tell her what
I knew and what I wanted to say, as well as what I *didn't* know, like why the
purple angora didn't bloom more after I washed it, so she wouldn't steer
the conversation into dangerous territory. She was genuinely curious, taking in what I had to say, fingering the swatches, sharing my surprises and
asking good questions. Sometimes, her eyes would go blank when I was in
the middle of explaining something. A few seconds later she'd nod, tap her
ear, and look back at me, "I'm sorry, what were you saying?"

Eunny wore a translucent earpiece that connected her to the control
room. Instructions were constantly being fed to her by not one but two
different people. Even during filming, while the cameras were rolling, she'd
get whispered words of counsel. Too slow? She'd nudge my leg. Too fast?
She'd nudge my leg. Did I say something wrong? She'd nudge my leg. I
became terrified of leg nudges.

Then the countdown would begin, "Five . . . four . . ." and a silent *three*,
two, and *one* in our heads. Eunny and I would gaze intently at something
on the table, smiling, heads bent in pretend conversation, before she'd
raise her head and toss a smile, "Welcome back!"

On our very first taping, she did her slick intro and threw it to me. I
got twenty words in before she tapped her ear, looked at the camera, and
said, "I'm sorry, we have to stop." What had I done?

"You said the name of the yarn," she said. Dammit.

My mind sprang to action. "If I can't say this is Harrisville yarn," I
asked, "can I say it was spun in Harrisville, New Hampshire?" After a
pause for deliberation, I was given an affirmative.

Cameras back on, we plowed through the rest of the episode in one
take. I looked at Eunny, waited for her eyes to lose that distant look. Finally,
word came through her earpiece, "We're good." Annie came in to take a

promotional picture of us with those samples before whisking them away
and replacing them with the next tray.

Sometimes Marilyn would come in and offer feedback or request a
reshoot. "That was great," she'd say, but usually it was more like, "Remember
to breathe," or "Try to watch the pace of your speech," or "We're picking up a
drumming noise whenever you pound the table." Once she silently unfolded
a note reminding us that our microphones were live and asking us to please
clean up our banter between takes. Just in case we still didn't understand,
she tapped on her chest where our microphones were pinned. We nodded.

The microphones would go off at lunch, the lab coats would be hung
up, and we'd head upstairs to a rooftop break area whose tinted sunroom
allegedly came from a Burger King that was being demolished. Meals
were brought in. Depending on the day, it was either taco salads, which put
everyone in a good mood, or Italian, which left us in a carb stupor for the
rest of the afternoon. Crew tended to eat with crew, office staff with office
staff, "talent" with support staff and producers.

Once the recycling was sorted and tables wiped clean, we'd return
downstairs to powder our faces, reapply our lipstick, spray our hair back
in place, don the next outfit, and resume shooting. My afternoons were
usually spent in the green room mainlining M&Ms and going over my
notes and swatches for the next day's taping, while the big screen showed
Eunny with a guest, or her crochet host, Kristin Omdahl, espousing steeks
or crochet edgings or any one of an endless supply of topics.

When all was done for the day, we'd pack our bags and pile back into
Marilyn's rental car for dinner. This being the suburbs and us being tired,
we'd usually head to one of the strip malls nearby. We'd go for Greek food
or to a burger joint with alcoholic milkshakes and big jugs of pickles—and,
always, at least one P.F. Chang's.

Dinnertime conversation was a lesson in diversity. Annie would tell
us about her latest fitness regime. ("I tried the Brazilian Butt-Lift, and
it lifted my butt, but now it's bigger!") They'd talk sports or dating, and
gradually Marilyn would steer us toward affordable healthcare or women's
reproductive rights. A waiter would appear and ask whose birthday it was.

We'd shake our heads, and he'd say, "Awesome, so it's just a ladies' night out, huh?"

Once, at P.F. Chang's, we did bother to explain that we were there on business, having finished a day of shooting a TV show for PBS. We had to explain what PBS was—"Yeah, like *Sesame Street*"—pointing to Eunny—"She's the host"—and Marilyn—"She's the producer." Unawed, he continued to call each of us "honey" for the rest of the night.

I'd leave them all shivering by the hotel door, Eunny and Annie puffing away. Marilyn would sometimes join them for her one cigarette of the year, pinching it between her fingers like Groucho Marx.

Collecting my complimentary chocolate-chip cookie in the lobby, I'd go up to my room and set the alarm extra early for the next day. As Eunny and I grew more comfortable with the segment, it took less and less time to shoot. Eventually, I only came for a few days. I always felt sad leaving them behind.

Filming *Knitting Daily TV* was some of the best fun I've ever had. I loved the pressure of the camera rolling, the tight constraints of subject matter, even the obscure PBS filming rules and not being allowed to look at the camera. It was like speed-dating through everything I knew and loved, with one hand duct-taped behind my back. More than that, I loved being part of a team.

I was there when Eunny signed off for her last episode before leaving Interweave, and I was there when Marilyn shook hands with the crew for the last time before she handed over the producer role to Karin Strom (who, too, has since left). I figured that transition was as good a time as any for me to hang up my lab coat, too, and let them reshape the show from scratch with a new host, new producer, new studio, segments, and crew.

I may not have won us an Emmy, but I did have a woman point at me once and exclaim, "Hey! You come on right after *Designing Women!*"

AUTUMN ON THE HUDSON:
Rhinebeck, New York

NESTLED ON THE EASTERN BANKS of the Hudson River, just
two hours north of Manhattan by train, is the picket-fenced village of
Rhinebeck. It has all the trappings of the weekend getaway: the artisanal
bread shop, reliable Thai food, a pricey French bistro, a high-end liquor
and wine store, and, to preserve an illusion of small-town America, a diner
with vinyl-upholstered booths and brusque waitresses.

In the fall, Rhinebeck becomes a Thornton Wilder vision of bucolic
small-town nostalgia. Between the foliage and the carved pumpkins on
porches, you can't help checking the local real estate ads and wondering
what it would be like to live here.

I think this every third weekend in October when I turn off the Taconic
State Parkway and wind my way into town for the New York State Sheep
and Wool Festival. So legendary is this show, it has attained Madonna or
Cher status in the knitting world. It is known by just one word: Rhinebeck.
Say that word to almost any knitter and you'll get a nod.

It's huge. Tens of thousands of people converge on the Dutchess
County Fairgrounds for two days of vending, demonstrations, workshops,
competitions, and get-togethers. The town of Rhinebeck and surrounding
villages along the Hudson come to a standstill on festival weekend, traffic
backing up for miles in every direction. For me, it's a return to my Upstate
New York childhood, to autumnal sights and smells for which I spent
years pining. I get to feast on still-warm donuts and tart apple cider, and,
most important of all, feel the comfort of being nestled among my kin.

The first show was held in 1972, one year before the similarly spirited
Maryland Sheep and Wool Festival got its start. Like Maryland, Rhinebeck
is sponsored by an agricultural group—the Dutchess County Sheep and
Wool Growers. But unlike its southern cousin, this show requires a paid

ticket to get in. Were it not for the ability to preorder your tickets online, I suspect we'd see people camped out overnight to get first dibs on the hottest vendors.

It all begins on Saturday morning, as cars quickly fill acres of grassy parking lots. Tour buses, chartered by faraway guilds and yarn shops, pull up and spill out knitters by the hundreds. They line up politely, single file, sometimes two at a time, smiling, talking, strategizing. The minute those gates finally open, the rush begins. Perfectly reasonable people break into a trot, then a sprint, in that fierce *I-have-a-plane-to-catch* kind of way, to get to their favorite booths before everyone else. (Knitters are kind and lovely people, but you don't want to get between them and their yarn.)

Every bed in town has been booked for months, sometimes years. The NO VACANCY signs extend up to Red Hook, down to Poughkeepsie, and across the Hudson to Newburgh. People trade rooms like drugs on the open market. "*Psssst,* I've got a double and only need one bed," you'll see the post on Ravelry. "Does anyone need a place to sleep?" Safety worries fly out the window as we snatch whatever we can, even if it means shacking up with a stranger.

Rhinebeck is best spent with friends, whether close or casual or even assembled just for the occasion. I first went in 2003 with my childhood friend Theresa, whom I'd only recently taught to knit. We stayed at a chain motel in Poughkeepsie and returned to our room each night like kids on Halloween, pouring the contents of our bags onto our beds to admire. Soon I returned with my *Knitter's Review* friends, this time staying at a newer chain motel in Newburgh. As our group grew larger and rowdier, we decided to rent a place just for us.

In 2009, we got cabins at the Mills-Norrie State Park, which occupies 1,000 prime acres along the Hudson just a few miles south of Rhinebeck. We drove in from every direction, me from Maine, Jen from Virginia, others from even farther afield, our cars laden with space heaters and blenders, toasters, extra lamps, and half the contents of a grocery store. We hiked in with our goods, setting up cabins better equipped than your average freshman dorm. Everything was idyllic . . . until we returned home on Saturday night to the news that we had no power. It had been shut off following an electrical short in the women's restroom. (Nobody had been hurt, although we did have particularly invigorating showers that morning.)

I wished my friends goodnight and stumbled through the pitch-black woods to my dark, freezing cabin. I locked the doors, covered myself in handknits, and shivered in my bunk bed, listening for the *rat-a-tat-tat* of Old Man Cooter's bloody stumps for fingers on my window.

The next year we rented a big house east of Rhinebeck. Not only was it haunted, we all agreed, but it sold soon after we left. So the following year we moved to a tiny farmhouse that had been remodeled so many times that it took us five minutes just to find the stairs leading to the second floor. We've since settled in a pretty home by the river, with its own indoor lap pool we all talk about but never use. If you go to Rhinebeck, or talk to those who do, you'll soon find that many people choose to rent houses with friends and make a slumber party of it.

Another festival tradition, sparked partly by climate and partly by crowd, is the so-called Rhinebeck sweater, which Ysolda Teague immortalized in her book of the same name. Mid-October in New York marks the beginning of sweater weather, and fewer venues offer as appreciative an audience as Rhinebeck. We plan our sweaters months ahead, picking our patterns and casting on. We go public with our projects, declaring our intents as sort of guarantees that we'll finish them in time. Friends cheer us on, goading, teasing, whatever it takes to get us to the final bind-off. Each sweater becomes such a community endeavor that, by the time we finally see a friend wearing hers in person, we can't help but feel like we played a part in its creation.

The last-minute rush to finish our Rhinebeck sweaters (and shawls, and socks, and . . . and . . .) inevitably means late blocking sessions on Friday night. The next morning, up and down the Hudson River, hotel housekeepers are baffled to find slightly damp beds that haven't been slept in. Who knows how many stray pins and darning needles have gone *tink-tink-tink* in their vacuum cleaners. By Sunday morning, the stranger things appear, like wads of what looks like wet sheep sitting on a towel in the bathroom—fleece samples handed to us by a friend and scoured in the sink before we went to bed.

The Rhinebeck dress code is pretty simple: If it's handknitted, you wear it. This is homecoming weekend for wool lovers, there's no holding back. For each of us, it all starts with a favorite sweater (if not a Rhinebeck sweater) over which a scarf is tossed. Maybe two. Plus a hat. Skirt? Why not? Don't forget mittens. Maybe a felted bag, too. Oh, and knitted socks, definitely. Would leg warmers be overkill? And so we stumble through the fairgrounds in our woolens like overburdened Christmas trees. But for this weekend, our passion is praised.

If a knitter is bringing family, naturally everyone is expected to represent. It's a joy to watch a knitter parade his or her kin through the fairgrounds. Babies in strollers are adorned from head to toe, carefully tucked in beneath colorful blankies. Husbands or wives dutifully wear elaborate Aran and Fair Isle creations that fit them perfectly. Even sulky teenage boys will acquiesce to wear, perhaps, a simple beanie.

The festival has its share of tire-kickers, too, those non-knitters who come to see what the fuss is all about. They stand out in their freshly pressed city-slicker attire, machine-knit sweaters, well-polished riding boots, and barn jackets that have never seen a barn. They often bring children who've never encountered livestock in any context other than on a restaurant menu. You'll see them crowded around the sheep-shearing demonstrations or lining the fence for the sheepdog trials. They cheer for the Leaping Llama contest and peruse books in the author's signing area, even though their contents are mysterious to them. Their willingness to take it all in is endearing.

For vendors, hundreds of whom compete for the 275 available spots, the weekend is about commerce. Staggering sums can change hands, tens of thousands of dollars per booth. Even in a slow year, the numbers are still remarkable. We hear of shoppers dropping more than $1,000 at a pop. The proximity to Manhattan works to everyone's advantage. These are among the best vendors in the country, selling to the most affluent.

The primary merchandise being sold is, of course, yarn. It spills from every aisle, in every texture and hue, machine-made and hand-spun, vat-dyed, hand-painted, and *au naturel*. Alongside the yarn are heaps of fleece and roving in equally varied shades from off-the-animal's-back to Technicolor. But also—and perhaps this is what distinguishes Rhinebeck the most from other shows—you'll find finished products galore. Not just mugs with sheep on them, but elegant hats, sweaters, socks, shearling booties, woven jackets, cheerful fabric aprons, and dresses made from repurposed wool sweaters. All are on hand for those who want to partake but have never knitted a stitch. People are still buzzing about the year Uma Thurman showed up and bought a pile of socks.

Part of the magic is the fairgrounds itself, 140 well-manicured acres of paved walkways snaking among some 20 barns, big and small. This is no dusty gravel affair; there's grass and mulched perennial beds and lovingly maintained trees that have managed to hold onto their most brilliant foliage just for us. You amble to the soundtrack of a Peruvian pan-flute band that plays along the main fairgrounds corridor. For years, we also had music from a hand-cranked hurdy-gurdy atop which perched a rather dejected stuffed monkey.

When mealtime arrives, you'll have to throw any aforementioned rules about festival food right out the window. This is the Hudson River Valley, my friends, the land of milk and honey and artisanal goat cheese. We're just a few miles up the road from the Culinary Institute of America. Sure, you'll still find fried dough, but here it comes in the form of airy and perfectly executed cider donuts rolled in cinnamon sugar and handed to you for a mere dollar. The falafel vendor is so good, you'll hear people talking in line about how it's even better than what they had in Beirut. By the time you get to the front of the artichoke line, the smell of garlic and white wine becomes so intoxicating, you're ready to eat your own arm.

The operative word here is *line*. Prepare to spend a lot of time in them. Rhinebeck is the place where you make "line friends," compatriots thrown together by chance, with whom you dedicate hours of your life in the pursuit of nourishment. Later, when you spot one another on the fairgrounds, yours is the greeting of old Army buddies. I still remember some of the people from the famous Chicken Pot Pie Line of 2007, which lasted just a little over two hours (no, I am not kidding) and had prompted such camaraderie, we could have formed our own village. Last year, a new pizza vendor had a ninety-minute waiting list ... to get on the waiting list. Non-knitting spouses and family members become vital pawns in the quest for food. Husbands and children are dispatched to monitor the lunch lines while knitters runs back to the barns to pursue those elusive skeins of yarn just one more time. Those who don't really care will shrug and be satisfied with a basket of limp french fries, a dyspeptic tub of lamb stew, a day-old cookie from one of the vendors with a shorter line. But for the really good food at Rhinebeck, follow the people.

You still have the occasional Fryolator novelties, the deep-fried pickle, the deep-fried spaghetti and meatballs, the deep-fried artichoke, but they're in the minority here. You'll also find fresh kettle corn, candied apples, buttery cakes, and flaky pastries, all accompanied by fresh apple cider or, perhaps, a more potent coffee or chai served, of course, in biode-gradable cups. Unlike Maryland Sheep and Wool, there are no lamb-only rules at Rhinebeck.

When the afternoon lull hits, you'll appreciate something that's very unique to Rhinebeck. In an exhibition building that's smack-dab in the center of everything, local vendors sell honey, breads and pastries, miles of cheeses, maple syrup, wines, and cordials. More than just selling them, they offer *samples* of them, making it possible to get slightly sloshed in the epicenter of sheep-and-wool nirvana. The pièce de résistance of the food building is the maple cotton candy, which is as delicious as it is entertaining. "Ooooh, what'd you get?" people ask, assuming I'll say Merino or maybe a blend of Cormo and silk. Instead, I shove a tuft of it in my mouth and chew.

This being a sheep-and-wool festival you will, of course, find sheep. The animal barns, however, make up far less of the focus here than they do at Maryland. Here, sheep provide more of a living museum than a significant marketplace. Yes, there's still showing and selling going on, but only two hours of formal selling and two hours of ribbon-awarding for the whole weekend. Otherwise, the animals perform a public service for those

city dwellers craving a connection with the country. "Say 'hi' to the sheep!"
I heard one woman tell her daughter, pointing a heavily jeweled finger at
an angora goat.

Besides the usual retail frenzy, Rhinebeck has a deeper frenetic energy
because it is the last big show of the year. While vendors are relieved, the
stakes are high for knitters. This marks our final opportunity to gather any
remaining nuts for the winter—by which I mean anything from a sweater's
worth of artisan yarn to, say, a spinning wheel, loom, or drum carder. Yes,
you can order those things online, but it just isn't the same.

I suspect Rhinebeck retains its charm, in part, because it is such a
fleeting experience. We wait for it all year, saving our pennies, planning
our sweaters, plotting our menus, scheduling time away from work, renting
rooms and houses, packing our cars. Then on Sunday afternoon when the
clock strikes 5:00 PM, a voice over the PA system tells us the show is closed.
Like with Cinderella and her magic pumpkin, the spell is broken. Even the
light on the fairgrounds seems to change the instant the gates shut.

Vendors whip into action, dismantling their booths in a fraction of the
time it took to set up. Part of me always feels just a wee bit hurt, like they
shouldn't be quite so eager to get out of there.

But hurry they must, in part because the organizers only give them a
few hours to disassemble. By the time the sun has passed over the horizon,
most of the vendor barns have been stripped. Only a few sheep remain to
reassure us a festival really did happen. Everything and everyone else has
been loaded back into cars, vans, trucks, and buses. Having given our last
hugs and said our goodbyes, we slowly fan out into the crisp fall evening,
headed for home.

MERRIMENT IN MINNETONKA

OCCASIONALLY YOU STUMBLE UPON a teaching venue that is so unusual, you feel compelled to return the next year just to experience it again—the adult version of getting off a carnival ride and immediately running back for another go.

I feel this way about Yarnover, a spectacular bash that has taken place in the Minneapolis area every spring since 1986. Teachers fly in from around the country—and not one or two teachers, but fifteen, a remarkable feat for an event with just one day to recoup its costs. Students pay over $100, more if they aren't yet guild members, to spend a full day at the show, which includes morning and afternoon classes and a boxed lunch. But this isn't strictly a profit-making venture. It's the annual gathering of a very big—as in more than 600 members—very active knitting guild representing the Twin Cities and Duluth. Nobody does knitting or knitting guilds quite like folks in cold, northern climates.

All the teachers arrive the day before, allowing us ample time to unpack and get a good night's sleep before our early wake-up call on Saturday morning. We line up at dawn in the hotel lobby, groggy-eyed and clinging to our coffees. Two small buses pull up out front. One by one, with suitcases of knitted samples in tow, swatches and sweaters and garments galore, we board. We zoom through freeways and neighborhoods before finally turning into a large Minnetonka parking lot, at the back of which sits a sprawling high school. It is ours for the day, the hallways and cafeteria and auditorium and classrooms.

There's something about entering a school, those long corridors, those shiny floors, that undeniable *school* smell, that gets me every time. Instantly, I regress. The banners and flyers announcing socials and proms; games and gatherings; contests, competitions, and campaigns, all written in that optimistic scrawl of high schoolers determined to break out of their one-horse town and make a name for themselves.

The hallways are chockablock with vendors who've been there since 7:45 AM setting up their booths for the day. Shelves are assembled, bins stacked, and lights mounted. Extension cords snake their way to the few available outlets in what can only be described as "creative power management." Fiber, yarns, needles, patterns, spinning wheels, accessories, and sample garments soon spill out into what has become a narrow and most distracting hallway. How surreal to walk down a crowded high school corridor, past the familiar drinking fountains and trophy cases and lockers, and see they've all been temporarily transformed into a knitting wonderland.

For two years in a row, I've been assigned the same room, a social-studies classroom with posters of Gandhi and Eleanor Roosevelt and Zora Neale Hurston, with inspirational quotes printed on white paper, glued onto colorful sheets of construction paper, and taped to the blank cinder-block walls. The chairs are bright orange, yellow, red, or blue, some kind of composite wooden material with the desk surface attached. The room is left as if the teacher heard us coming, put down her coffee, and ran—her mug right there, still half full, on the desk with sticky notes, the crumpled silver foil of a Hershey's Kiss, an uncapped ballpoint pen.

I greet the early arrivals and begin to unpack, listening to the squeak of shoes in the hallway, the echo of voices. We're at the end of a long and potentially confusing corridor, and the knitters, innately distracted by the presence of yarn and fiber, take their time to arrive. Finally, I count the people, count the names on my list, mentally *tut-tut* the laggards, and close my classroom door—over which a black-and-white Che Guevara poster is taped.

I take attendance and begin explaining how we will tackle the world of twist and ply in just three hours—then the doorknob rattles. In comes the first latecomer, out of breath, gasping apologies. "Not to worry; take your seat," I say, checking her off the attendance list. A few minutes later, in come two more stragglers, both carrying several bags of yarn from the marketplace. Guilt is written all over their faces. I cross off their names. Not until we're deep into that first hour does the last laggard saunter in, the knitting version of Sean Penn's character from *Fast Times at Ridgemont High*. She shows no guilt, gives no apology, just nods while taking her sweet time getting settled. I make a special mark next to her name. Problem student. By mid-semester, I'll probably be calling in her parents for a meeting.

As class continues, I flash back to the teachers I watched from my own uncomfortable chair many years ago. How I studied their speech, their mannerisms, even the way they used their chalk, some preferring fresh, long pieces, others breaking off little nubbins. I admired their confidence and authority. I wanted to be one of them. Now, my back to the class, talking while writing notes about properties of wool on the board, I have that eerie feeling of having slipped into the skin of those very teachers. I am Mrs. Serkowski, jotting her equations; I am Mr. Geiss, expertly diagramming sentences. Only I'm not; I'm Clara, writing words like *crimp* and *staple* and *micron*, diagramming twist and ply.

Occasionally, we are interrupted by laughter from the room next door—which has also been occupied, for two years running, by fellow teacher and extraordinarily funny person Amy Detjen. I have to break up a whispered conversation between two students seated in back. Someone raises her hand and asks to use the restroom. I nod. Does anybody else need to go? Hands shoot up. We declare a ten-minute break that becomes a fifteen-minute break as the last student returns, laden with bags of yarn, another casualty of the marketplace.

We proceed through our lesson. The students are nimble. They keep pace, sometimes slipping ahead and asking questions that lead, as if on cue, to where I was about to go next. It's a beautiful morning. We finish just as the stomach growls begin. Some sprint to the marketplace or the lunch line. Others linger to ask questions. A few offer to help me sort and stack swatches. Finally, they're gone, I take a big breath, wipe off the blackboard, store my belongings, and go in search of lunch.

The long cafeteria line moves swiftly. We have a choice of sandwiches: ham, turkey, roast beef, or, for the vegetarians, cheese. I pick a white paperboard box marked TURKEY, grab a bottle of water, and look for a place to sit. I spot a few familiar faces, but their tables are full. "Sorry," they mouth silently before turning back to their groups. I keep walking past tables of friends, insular circles, all staring at me. I spot two strangers at a big table. "May I join you?" They nod. I sit down and smile. They leave. I eat my lunch in silence.

In addition to my turkey sandwich on white bread, with mustard and mayo packets on the side, I have a small bag of Lay's potato chips, a bright red apple, and, in its own paper pocket, a chocolate-chip cookie. Extra napkins are at the bottom of the box. I'm wondering why my mother hasn't packed my usual thermos of Progresso Lentil Soup or leftover Chinese food when I glance at my watch and realize I have to get to class.

By the time I get back to my classroom, a few new eager beavers have already arrived. One has put an apple on my desk (I mentally put a star next to her name on the attendance list). Others are politely pawing through my swatches and samples, unable to resist the lure of a heap of handknits.

The afternoon is a replay of the morning, until a great lethargy over-takes the group at about 3:00 PM. Eyes glaze over. Eleanor's gaze has taken on a disapproving tone. Zora isn't even talking to us anymore. "You think that's good spinning?" Gandhi seems to be asking as he deftly demon-strates how cotton *really* should be spun. I hear the clock's faint *tick, tick, tick* over the drone of an annoying noise I realize is, in fact, my own voice. I eye that cold, half-drunk mug of coffee.

Finally, the bell rings and class is dismissed. Some are out of there like a shot, hoping to make one more pass at the marketplace on their way out. Others line up with questions or comments, with lovely stories, or with one of my books to sign. Some bring mystery skeins ("Could you tell me what this is?") or bags of fiber from their sheep, or their friend's sheep, or their friend's dead grandmother's sheep, hoping I can identify it, or, at a minimum, praise them for having the foresight to keep it all these years. The apple giver is now at my table, carefully stacking my swatches and samples, matching them according to size, slipping them into the bags and packing them into my suitcase without my having had to ask. I mentally give her an A for the semester.

We have fifteen minutes to pack up and get out of school before the clock strikes 4:45 PM. I move the chairs back into place, give the chalkboard one final swipe, return the half-drunk mug of coffee to its rightful place on the desk. There is no time to dally or I'll miss my ride home.

The wheels of my suitcase make forlorn squeaking sounds on the polished linoleum floor. Once-animated classrooms are now dark and empty, the vendors packed up and gone. Out front, the bus idles impatiently, waiting for the last of the teachers to climb in.

That night we will gather again at the hotel, just the teachers, for a celebratory dinner in a meeting room right off the indoor swimming pool. Over plates of chicken Florentine, steamed broccoli, and rice pilaf, we'll exchange notes. The main topics of conversation: how lovely the students were, what a rare event this is, and at what exact time in the afternoon did each of us grow tired of our own voices. Nods all around. One person insists this never happens to her because what she's teaching is so exciting and her students are so amazing. Somewhat deflated, we return to small talk over slices of pie.

I relish the surreal state of time travel while it lasts, feeling part teenager, part a grown-up version of my favorite teachers. I go to bed resolved: The next morning, I'll break out of that one-horse town and make a name for myself. Really, I will.

STASH-WRANGLING IN THE MILE-HIGH CITY: Denver

'TWAS THE WEEK BEFORE CHRISTMAS when I flew to Denver to film a class for the online learning platform Craftsy. Founded in 2010 and launched in 2011, this heavily funded start-up has capitalized on the market for online craft instruction. They've plucked top names from the teaching circuit, capturing their best classes and extending them to a vast and eager virtual audience. Their rise has been meteoric.

This was my second time at Craftsy. My first class—called "Know Your Yarn," all about, as you might guess, the structure and properties of different yarns—had done so well that they'd invited me back for a repeat performance. But where do you go after a class about yarn? My answer was a class about *dealing with* yarn. That is, managing your yarn stash so that it remains a source of inspiration rather than overwhelm.

My new class, which I'd privately nicknamed "Hoarders: The Knitting Edition," would be called "Stashbusting." In seven fifteen-minute video lessons filmed over the course of three days, I would gently hold people's hands as they faced their excesses and let go. We would get organized, tackle unfinished projects, identify oddballs, and use up precious leftovers in several stash-busting projects before putting everything away for safekeeping.

It was midday when my plane landed in a bleak Siberian landscape of drifting snow, Denver having just gotten its first dusting of the season. Luckily, Craftsy sends a driver to meet you at the airport and get you safely to your hotel. My driver was John, a man who wore a leather bomber jacket, had a rattling smoker's cough, and enjoyed talking about weather patterns.

Accustomed to shuffling Craftsy teachers back and forth each week, John asked what I was teaching. I explained the concept of my class to him, and he nodded sagely. "Inventory management," he said.

A flashy new hotel had been built since my last visit, and Craftsy had booked it for my stay. The lobby looked like the set of a 1960s game show, with brightly colored swiveling pod chairs and glowing orbs suspended from the ceiling. Behind the front desk, someone was playing with a yo-yo. Each floor had been given its own theme (One-Hit Wonders, Big Hair, Mad About Music, etc.) complete with a jingle that played when you got off the elevator. I was on the Dance Floor. My room had a massive print of a woman wearing an ice-cream cone on her head.

Next door, the *Nutcracker* matinee was just getting out at the Denver Center for the Performing Arts. Families were streaming by in their holiday finest, girls with ribbons in their hair, little boys in suits. The sun was setting as I slurped my requisite bowl of pho at a nearby Vietnamese restaurant, washing it down with a cherry lollipop on my way back to the hotel. By 9:00 PM, downtown Denver was a ghost town.

The next morning at 7:30 AM sharp, moderately rested and fully breakfasted, I met two other women in the lobby. We were all strangers to one another, but they were here to teach fabric-related classes. We were retrieved by a tiny, sweet-voiced makeup artist named Danica, whose claim to fame is that her brushes have touched both President Obama *and* Tyra Banks. Her car would carry us to the Craftsy studio.

It's hard to believe that this vaunted hub for online craft learning was founded by four guys who've never knit or sewn a stitch. John Levisay and Josh Scott met at eBay, where they worked together managing the resale of cars and industrial equipment. In 2010, along with buddies Todd Tobin and Bret Hanna, both ServiceMagic alums, they raised around $6 million in venture capital to launch a new e-school platform called Sympoz, Inc. Their idea was to offer online classes on "serious" subjects like finance, wine appreciation, and preparing for fatherhood. They added a beginner quilting class and were surprised when it sold three times faster than the others. Smart enough to perceive a trend, they promptly nabbed an additional $15 million in venture capital and spun off a vertical unit, called Craftsy, that would focus on providing high-quality classes on "crafty" topics like quilting, knitting, and cake decorating. By 2013, Craftsy was bringing in $23 million in revenue. It's easy to make sweeping gender generalizations about the target audience, and even harder to refute them: The majority of Craftsy students are women.

Since my first visit, the company had swelled to 200 employees. News was buzzing about a fresh $50 million they were getting from a new investor. It meant they would soon be hiring seventy more people. Knitting, quilting, and cake decorating remained the core subjects, with a recent management directive to launch one new class per week in each of those subjects. Meanwhile, they were also feeding a healthy base of classes on other subjects, from cooking and photography to woodworking, gardening, and jewelry-making.

Such growth meant I wasn't the only one filming a workshop that week. As Danica drove, I learned more about my fellow teachers. Riding shotgun with Danica was the self-titled minister of corrections at the Chicago School of Fusing, here to teach a class on something she called "fusible collage." Sitting in back with me was a widowed and soon-to-be-grandmother quilter from Utah, here to present a class based on one of her popular quilted pillow patterns. A busy staff of Craftsy acquisitions editors constantly seeks out new talent to bring into town and capture on screen.

Just a minute or two beyond downtown in an otherwise flat, industrial area, we crossed over a river packed with geese. Like sailboats, they all pointed upwind against the current. A few seconds later we pulled into the parking lot.

Craftsy films its workshops at Taxi, a 25,000 square-foot cinderblock building that used to house Yellow Cab. From the outside, it still looks like the kind of place where you'd see a Danny DeVito type yelling orders from his dispatcher's cage. Inside, the cars have been replaced by offices, of which Craftsy rents a corner for its studio. Everything is filmed here, but the remaining work—turning videos into classes, then selling and support-ing them—takes place at corporate headquarters downtown.

I was pointed to an empty dressing room with a slate star on the door, on which my name had been written. Beyond my dressing room, an art studio stood empty, its cloudy faux-garret windows evoking a gritty urban artist's space. The last time I was here, a man from Philadelphia was filming a drawing class in that studio. I remember getting out of my shoot just in time to catch his crew presenting him with a big chocolate birthday cake, candles and all.

In the hallway, prop shelves held Styrofoam heads and posable mannequins, cans of fixative and spray starch, and endless plastic boxes of fabric and yarns and gadgets that'd come in handy for one of the 600-plus classes filmed here since the beginning. The cinderblock hallway was lined in eggshell foam to cushion ambient noise.

The studio where I would film my class was still quiet, just a jumble of lights, cameras, and assorted props. Perched on a director's chair with her tea and her iPhone was my producer, Cara. She'd recently left Craftsy to follow her ceramics-professor boyfriend to Nebraska and work on her real passion, which was writing screenplays. But every few weeks, she'd make the eight-hour drive back to Denver to produce classes as a freelancer. People kept coming in and giving her hugs.

The studio is set up so that you stand at a table with a camera directly in front of you, a second camera to the side (for swoop-ins and "Oh, I didn't see you there!" greetings to your imaginary students), and a third camera overhead to capture your hands working stitches or pointing, oh so elegantly, at something on the table. A microphone is pinned somewhere on your front, with a cord discretely running down your back to a transmitter clipped to your waist or tucked into a pocket.

Your producer sits behind the main camera, observing everything as it happens. Her job is to keep you on track, making sure you follow the course outline and touch on all the previously agreed-upon points—without saying or doing anything wrong.

Seated at a table behind the producer is the switcher. This person is tasked with watching the feeds from each camera and seamlessly switching from feed to feed, angle to angle, as the class unfolds. Doing this now helps speed up the after-shoot production work, which, in turn, helps Craftsy achieve that ambitious weekly class launch schedule. My switcher, Andrew, wandered in. This bearded musician and composer had shot my last class and, in his spare time, performs in a band called Skein.

At last, a tall, smiling scarecrow of a man came in and introduced himself as Rob. Our cameraman, he had moved here from California with his wife and occasionally played what he called "heavy cello" for Skein. They were all friends, and they all had interesting hobbies. In fact, spend any time at the Craftsy studios and you'll quickly see that everyone here has another passion, be it writing or acting, storytelling or stand-up comedy. For me, it was like a reunion with people I loved in high school drama club. "So *this* is where they all ended up!" I thought.

After a quick visit to Danica's room to have years of fatigue and exasperation wiped from my face, it was time to set up the studio and lay down our first class. Only it's not a class, it's a *lesson*. Craftsy has its own jargon that corresponds to an underlying technology platform that is powerful but inflexible.

The Craftsy format keeps shifting, but as of this writing, one class is composed of seven lessons, each approximately fifteen to twenty minutes long. While the class can theoretically be played like a movie, chapter by chapter, from start to finish, students often pop in and out of lessons in random order. Because of this, you're discouraged from making any linear references, like "coming up!" or "in our last lesson," when you speak. You'll get a raised hand from your producer, which is Craftsy talk for "CUT!"

Cara and I went over the premise for the first lesson, the key points I was to convey. Normally, you begin with the second lesson and only film the first when you've found your pace, but we decided to be bold and start at the beginning. I pointed myself to one camera, then another. I posed my hands in front of me to make sure they were framed properly by the camera above my head. We repeated this until all the important shots were framed just right.

"Just try not to flail your hands," were the instructions. "We're getting a glare from your glasses, could you tuck your head down just a little?" "Can you move an inch to the right?" "Your hair is touching the microphone, can you keep it off your shoulder?" "Make sure the yarn doesn't go beyond this mark or else it'll be out of the frame." And, of course, "Smile!

Relax!" I could feel a trickle of sweat run down my back.

With those instructions and a dozen more, and with a brain full of words I needed to convey in precise order, we gave it a try.

In addition to standing one inch to the right of the transparent piece of tape on the table, while keeping my head tucked down just a little and not moving my hands in any flail-like manner, I also had to say, in an impromptu-styled conversational tone, three precise takeaways that people would learn from that workshop, only it wasn't called a *workshop*, it was called a *class*, and each class had *lessons*, and I found it all impossible to keep straight. "In this workshop," I began my introduction, "I'm going to teach you how to sort, weed, and prune your stash until only—"

My producer raised her hand. "I'm sorry but you said 'in this workshop' when it's really 'in this *class*,' can we try again?" I tried again, but this time I got the raised hand for saying "Coming up next" instead of "In Lesson Two."

During a brief break, I was asked a question that would be repeated at least every hour during my stay: "Are you drinking enough water?"

That is the most important question for anyone visiting Denver, whether you're there to shoot a Craftsy class or just twiddle your thumbs in a hotel room. Here in the mile-high city, altitude is your invisible foe. The air is so much thinner and drier that visitors are instructed to drink twice as much water as they would back home.

With its weekly influx of teachers flying in from elsewhere, Craftsy takes the water prescription very seriously. I was told of a teacher who forgot to drink for a day and ended up in the hospital. And so, between takes, I pulled out a water bottle and sipped from a straw so as not to mar the thick paste of pink lipstick on my mouth.

Lunches are a communal affair at Craftsy. Each day, food is trucked in from an area restaurant—and each day, the restaurant changes. One day it might be a selection of funky salads, the next day, a pasta bar, or thick sandwiches with layers of strange and delicious ingredients. Meals are set out on a table in the Craftsy kitchen and everyone gets to pick what they want.

The Craftsy kitchen is stocked as if by a nine-year-old given a credit card and set free in Whole Foods. I found chocolate-covered bananas, peanuts, apricots, and raisins; bags of plain and peanut M&Ms; every kind of granola bar and chewy chocolate-caramel bar; tidy wrapped squares of Ghirardelli chocolate; snack bags of gourmet chips and popcorn; and a drink machine that spat out bottles for free. You just pushed a button for whatever you wanted and it came tumbling out. The drinks were mostly naturally sweetened, vitamin-infused pink or yellow "health waters," but garbage could still be found. When we came up one lunch short, Andrew insisted on foraging. "I'll just put together a little charcuterie plate," he said. It was, on closer examination, two packages of string cheese, a handful of pretzels, a few stubby Slim Jims, and a side bowl of popcorn.

We carried our food out to the communal dining area in the open corridor running the length of the building. Everyone at the Craftsy studios eats together at a big colorful table here. More tables are claimed by tenants from other offices. We sat down with my Utah quilter, her producer, and her crew and compared notes on our morning shoots. Occasionally, we'd laugh too loud and someone would tiptoe out of a nearby Craftsy studio to shush us.

We made it through four lessons that day, which was a record both for me and the crew. The next day was a repeat of the previous one, the 7:30 AM wake-up call, Danica and the others in the lobby, light chatter in the car. This time my crew and I hit our pace and managed to end early in the afternoon, which—despite the increasingly sped-up pace of things at Craftsy—was still uncommon. I overheard Cara telling this to others (coming in to give her more hugs) and there was always a pause then a "Really?"

I worried that our speedy shoot was actually a bad sign, that I'd been too sloppy or skipped essential points, but Cara's outline was covered with checkmarks, so I had to trust.

Our early dismissal gave Andrew plenty of time to get to his young daughter's trombone recital, while Rob could clean his cameras and dismantle the equipment in preparation for his next shoot. The crew never rests. Tomorrow, they would be shaking hands with a new teacher. As for me, I repacked my samples, folded up all my clothes, and gave a parting glance to my perfect, painted face in the mirror. I would scrub it off later that night.

It's hard not to be swept up into a sense of stardom when you're at Craftsy, with that limo at the airport, the star on your dressing-room door, being tended to by a makeup artist, having someone fuss over your lighting and microphone. It's very, very easy to forget why you're there: to teach.

You want to be engaging and entertaining while you do it, but you're there to convey carefully organized facts about which you are a presumed expert. As much as it's helpful to smile as you deliver a flub-free speech, what you say must follow a very specific predetermined outline and deliver key promised learning objectives.

For weeks leading up to the shoot, teachers work with a producer to fine-tune their workshops (dammit, not workshops, *classes*) until they fit the organizational constraints of the Craftsy platform hand in glove. Your subject needs to fit into a predetermined number of lessons, each lesson needing to fill a specific number of minutes, and each lesson needs to satisfy three specific learning objectives. Once you're in the studio and the cameras are rolling, you have to follow that outline, point by point, without running over or under. The clock is ticking, and when your time is up, your crew is immediately due elsewhere.

Producers are not—and cannot possibly be expected to be—experts in every subject they oversee. And here's where the Craftsy method may have one flaw. As a teacher, without students to nod or shake their heads and ask questions, and with the added pressure of bright lights and keeping your head down and not flubbing your so-called lines, it's a challenge to stay focused and feel confident you're doing a good job. And when a producer says, "That looked good to me," they may be talking about certain mechanics and not about what the class itself really needs.

The first time I was at Craftsy, I was lucky to be paired with a producer who was a knitter. This time, help came in the form of my switcher Andrew. If you hadn't guessed from the name of his band, Andrew is an avid knitter. Between shots, he'd come over with a skein and ask me questions about it. After a tricky shot, where I tried to explain how to work a triangle-shaped stashbuster shawl from the top down, he shook his head at the producer's thumbs-up, and we reshot, several times, until it made sense to him. Which definitely made the class better. (As a thank-you, I left him with a skein of Artyarns silk and mohair so he could make a similar shawl for his mother-in-law.)

Maybe I'm overthinking things. For the thousands of students who may register for a single class, only a small percentage actually completes them. Like cookbooks and gym memberships, class purchases tend to be aspirational. A class can have six or seven thousand registered students and only a few dozen actively posting in the discussion area or leaving questions for the teacher.

Having finished a whole day early, I thought it only fair to visit Craftsy headquarters, especially since they were just a few blocks from my hotel. The corporate offices occupied most of the second floor of a shiny skyscraper connected by covered walkway to the Ritz-Carlton. If the studio was filled with the drama-club people, the offices were where everyone else in high school had ended up—jocks and geeks and cheerleaders alike.

It was like a film set for an Internet start-up. The open space had acres of long white tables divided by low frosted-glass panels to give a vague illusion of privacy. People sprawled on plush Scandinavian-style chairs and couches in a dimly lit "Relaxation Lounge," each face illuminated by the glowing screen of a MacBook. Meeting rooms had glass walls. The only privacy was in little phone closets tucked around the floor, but even those had large windows and dubious soundproofing. As if following my thoughts, many people sported some form of noise-cancelling earphones. With few exceptions, they all seemed to be millennials.

I passed a woman, seated with her back to me, who was staring at two screens where the "me" from yesterday was talking. She was editing my class. I tapped her on the shoulder. "Boo!" After filming is complete, they move through production quickly, finishing the bulk of it by the end of the week. Next comes graphics and illustrations, the opening music and voiceover introduction. While the marketing and publicity departments begin their work, other staff goes in, watches the class, and populates the platform with "seed questions," designed to make it feel active. I, in turn, go in and answer the questions to encourage discussion among students.

Back at the Craftsy office I started to notice toy weaponry scattered on desks and tables, Nerf guns mostly. Apparently, they were there to help people blow off steam. "Yeah," one person told me with the raised eyebrow of a non-believer. "You never know when a battle will break out." At the reception desk, I spotted what looked like a large stuffed dog. Around its neck, a sign proclaimed, "I'm a cake!" All the food-related leftovers from class shoots end up here.

That night, I met up with Eunny Jang, by then an acquisitions editor at Craftsy, for dinner. Years ago, at age twenty-three, the blogger had been tapped to succeed Pam Allen as editor of *Interweave Knits*. Once the wunderkind of the knitting world, she had since left the magazine to work for the sewing division of Craftsy—and when we met for dinner, she was still coming to grips with her recent thirtieth birthday. Over plates of pierogies at a bar downtown, she told me that the Craftsy corporate culture was making even *her* feel old.

Early the next morning, a new limo pulled up for my ride to the airport. Gone was John. This time, my driver was a young and soft-spoken yet outgoing woman named Betsy. She wore an old-fashioned chauffeur's hat.

As we sped through the darkness, she explained that this driving gig was just something she did to fill the time and make extra cash. She liked the people. She'd worked at a yarn store, but recently her passion had turned more to sewing. In fact, she'd begun teaching sewing classes to young girls.

"Isn't it scary to put such young people in front of sewing machines?" I asked, thinking of my nieces and their once-tiny fingers.

"Oh no," she told me. "They're great. We do really simple things, like pillowcases, to help them build confidence and develop basic sewing skills."

She navigated a tricky freeway merge and then went on, "I love it. I feel like I'm helping them learn so much more than just sewing, like about patience and linear thinking." She glanced over her shoulder and changed lanes. "I had this one girl who just couldn't concentrate for long, and I'd watch her start to slip. So I took her aside and said, 'I know this part is bor-ing, but if you don't complete this part, you don't get to do the *next* part, which isn't boring.' And she actually got it!"

My decision to teach classes online with Craftsy had been mostly a selfish one: By presenting the very best version of my class on an interactive, easy-to-use platform, I could reach more people without ever boarding a plane—and still make my mortgage payment. But here was a foot soldier doing the real work, teaching a group of young girls the old-fashioned way. Not only did these kids benefit from a teacher who could make split-second adjustments to suit the group dynamic, but they were enjoying the group dynamic itself—the joy of discovering something tactile and communal together.

No matter how slick the technology or charming the person on screen, I don't think we'll ever be able to replicate the full extent of the human learning experience online. Nor should we. There's a time for sit-ting at home in your pajamas, watching and clicking and quietly forming connections in your mind. And there's a time for getting out and being with others, for reaching into the picture and becoming part of it.

CASHMERE DREAMS AND BRITISH BREEDS: A Last-Minute Visit to Edinburgh, Scotland

EDINBURGH HAD NEVER BEEN at the top of my must-see list. London, definitely, with a swing down to see the sheep farms around Devon. But if it hadn't been for the Edinburgh Yarn Festival, I'd probably still be ignorant about this distinguished little capital city with its Medieval Old Town, an extinct volcano, and a castle at its peak.

It was only in its second year, but the Edinburgh Yarn Festival's transformation from 2014 to 2015 was enough to suggest the hallmarks of impending greatness. Big things were happening for knitters all across the United Kingdom as the country—along with much of Europe—was finally enjoying its own long-awaited knitting boom.

I'd been in London in 2010 and 2011 for an event called Knit Nation. It, too, foretold greatness—but most of the teachers had been flown in from the States and Canada, and many of the students were either North American expats or very well-traveled Brits. Even the organizers were from away, Cookie A from the United States, Alice Yu from Canada but married to a Brit. At that time, just a few yarn stores offered anything beyond the international brands. Breed-specific wool, although in a country renowned for its breeds, was still rare. Classes like mine on the construction of yarn and qualities of breed-specific wool were a little on the fringe. Most British farmers were piling their fleeces in a heap and burning them for lack of a market. But the line outside the first Knit Nation marketplace suggested which way the winds would soon blow. Just a few years later, Edinburgh was sprouting its own, very much homegrown, festival—and I wanted to be there to witness it.

After a restless night on the transatlantic flight, I finally spotted lights below. Just a few faint flickerings like the ones I imagine people spotting when their planes make landfall over my tiny Maine town. Then, a blush of pinkish blue on the horizon followed by intense clusters of golden dots. The land gave way to jetties, with long, illuminated roads snaking out to small islands like lollipops.

In the distance, I saw another shoreline and more lights before clouds swallowed us. At 167 miles to Edinburgh, we tipped our nose down, the engine lowered to a purr, and we began our final descent. The female flight attendants had removed their ballet flats and were back in their patent-leather pumps. Rick, their smooth-voiced male counterpart, had removed his apron and donned a crisp navy blazer with wings pinned on the lapel. Six minutes to go, I watched the final stragglers make for the bathroom.

At immigration, a plump, ruddy-cheeked woman gestured me forward.

"Reason for your visit?" she asked.

"I'm here to play," I smiled.

"You're a tourist," she corrected me.

"Yes, yes, I'm here as a tourist."

It was at this precise location, or thereabouts, that several US nationals had been waylaid just five years ago on their way to the first (and last) UK Knit Camp. Problems with work visa paperwork resulted in nail-biting days of negotiating and, in the case of one teacher, an unexpected return flight to the United States. With that history still fresh in my mind, I didn't mention the words *yarn* or *knitting* to this woman for fear she'd drag me into a room and interrogate me. She smiled, typed something into her system, handed me back my passport, and wished me a nice stay.

It was barely 7:00 AM and the small airport was still waking up. I made my way outside and to the tram stop, where a shiny new tram would whisk me the twenty minutes to town. Like most European cities, Edinburgh has a large and efficient public transit system. Bigger routes have the double-decker buses and all offer free Wi-Fi—helpful if, like me, you're an international traveler with no roaming plan.

Already my credit card wasn't working.

"You Americans are always in a rush," giggled the young woman who'd come over to help me at the ticket machine. "You just have to leave the card in there for a moment. . . ." We stared at the machine in silence, and this time it worked. I tried to explain that our machines yell at us if we don't remove our cards fast enough.

The tram closed its doors and headed for town. The sun was now rising on a wonderfully wet, dreary landscape of muddy fields, bare trees, gray skies, and emerald-green grass. Gradually, flat office parks and suburban shopping malls replaced the empty fields. We passed the hulking black metal skeleton of Murrayfield Stadium, its parking lot still empty. Garbage was scattered along the tram line, plastic bags fluttered in the bushes. At each stop, tired commuters got on, took their seats, and stared blankly at their smartphones. Schoolchildren swayed and chattered in lovely Scottish accents.

Travel lends a glow that makes liars of us all. Here was the same gray day that drives me to despair in Maine, the same garbage and mud and crowds of baggy-eyed sniffers on public transportation, and yet here I rejoiced in how *romantically dreary* it all was. "Travel is a state of mind," explained writer Paul Theroux. "It has nothing to do with existence or the exotic. It is almost entirely an inner experience." I suspect life is 97 percent attitude and only 3 percent actual experience. How else can it be that I drink the same tea every morning—made with the same water, in the same cup—and yet it tastes better on certain days, worse on others? The same seat on a plane feels different during takeoff and landing depending on whether I'm coming or going.

I got off the tram at Haymarket Station, a bustling stop just a few minutes from central Edinburgh. Checking my map, I started walking toward my hotel. At each intersection I gave myself whiplash looking right, left, right, left, then giving up and running for dear life across the street. I couldn't quite believe the "Look Right" markings on the road because everything in my cellular make-up said that traffic *should* be coming from the left.

Suitcase clattering on the sidewalk, I turned down a side street and spotted a familiar figure: Ysolda Teague on her bike, wearing an old tweed jacket, wool shorts, thick tights, and paint-splattered leather shoes, waiting for me. My hotel being not too far from her home, we'd made plans to meet for breakfast—plans firmed up, I might add, thanks to that free Wi-Fi on the tram. It was too early to check in at my hotel, so I left my suitcase with the front desk and we started walking. "It's hard to find any place that's open before eight o'clock that isn't a Starbucks," she explained, as we made our way, bicycle between us, to a place fittingly called Milk.

I've known Ysolda since she made her first knitting trek to the United States in 2009. She was barely in her twenties then, gutsily piecing together an unprecedented, months-long teaching tour on the fly. This young designer relied on the kindness of guild members, friends of shop owners, and strangers met over the Internet to get her safely from one place to the next. She surfed her way across some of the finest couches and guest rooms of North America, forming friendships that endure to this day. "How else would I have met Jess and Casey?" she said, referring to Jessica and Casey Forbes, the founders of Ravelry.

"I wouldn't do it now," she added, glancing up from her bowl of muesli. "No way." In the decade that had passed since that first tour, the Scottish designer has matured into a levelheaded businesswoman. But the fearlessness remains, the willingness to try anything. Until Ysolda, nobody had even thought to investigate the feasibility of bringing an Airstream trailer onto the TNNA show floor. ("Totally possible," she said.)

This fearlessness, combined with a refusal to accept orders from anyone else, has left Ysolda in a tricky situation for one so young: Having gone straight from college to running her own business, she likes to point out that she's never had a real job. "I'm pretty much unemployable."

One major growing-up milestone she has yet to achieve is getting her driver's license. "It's the only thing I can't teach myself," she told me. "I'd much rather go to an old airfield, prop a book on the steering wheel, and figure it out on my own."

Instead, she rides her bike across Edinburgh every day to reach a new studio space that's double the size of her previous one. Her bike is beautiful and substantial, built by a man who also knits. "He's very minimalist," Ysolda explained. "He has one hat, one sweater. When he's done knitting a project, he unravels it and starts over."

It would be easy to say part of Ysolda's success was just timing. She had never even seen a copy of *Vogue Knitting* or *Interweave Knits* before her first pattern was published online. She rose entirely through the ranks of newcomers, meeting other designers (including up-and-comers Eunny Jang and Stefanie Japel) on a site called Craftster. In 2005, she discovered the online knitting magazine *Knitty*, then just three years old.

"I wouldn't be here if it weren't for *Knitty*," she said. "They made it look really easy to submit a design, so I did." She was nineteen when her first pattern—a cardigan called Arisaig—was published. "I had no idea there was a person called a technical editor," she said. "I just charted out each stitch on graph paper." Ysolda didn't even have a blog yet. That began after *Knitty* asked for her bio and said, "Oh, by the way, this is a great place to link to your blog." Her pattern appeared on the cover of *Knitty*, and overnight, her blog traffic spiked into the tens of thousands of readers. They asked where they could find more patterns by her, and she responded accordingly.

You could say that Ysolda had the good fortune to enter the scene when *Knitty* was still in its infancy, and rise just as Ravelry was clearing a runway for independent knitwear designers. But personality, skill, and persistence were equally key.

Ysolda's decision to sell her patterns herself at a fair price—in those days, around six dollars per pattern—instead of handing over all the rights to a publisher or yarn company in exchange for a few hundred dollars was a game changer for the industry. She was also among the first to offer her patterns as downloadable PDFs rather than as printed leaflets—which she did mostly because of her geographic remoteness.

Historically, knitting patterns have been provided free, or at greatly subsidized prices, by yarn companies to help sell yarn. More recently, designers had to hustle to make a living, spreading their work across yarn companies, books, and magazines whenever the opportunity presented itself. But nearly always, the rights to their work were lost in the process.

Ysolda still remembers her first TNNA show, when the owner of a major yarn company stood, dumbstruck, in her booth.

"What do you do?" he had asked.

"I sell patterns," she answered.

"Yes, but what's your *business*?" he asked again, unable to conceive of a business model built around patterns alone.

It's her same sense of "why not?" fearlessness that inspired her to book a booth at this year's Handarbeit, the handcrafts and hobby trade show in Cologne, Germany, that has been long considered the exclusive domain of men in suits. Even without seeing it, I knew the impact Ysolda's booth would have. Her spaces are charming, cozy cottages of cardigans and twinkle lights, baby sweaters and colorful shawls. Before showtime, she is in boots and overalls, wielding a drill with the skill of a teamster. But once the doors open, all you see is warmth and charm.

Only a fool would mistake that outward softness for weakness, the prettiness for a lack of acumen. She is smart, stubborn, shrewd, and unafraid to go after what she wants. Ysolda marches to a drumbeat entirely her own.

When she was a child, she came home from school one day and complained to her mother that nobody would talk to her.

"You should go up and talk to them," her mother had advised, to which Ysolda responded, "No, they should come to *me*."

We'd left the restaurant and were walking along a busy street now, Ysolda pushing her bike, me racing to keep up. Suddenly, the buildings parted to my right and I saw a deep wooded gully, on the other side of which rose a steep hill with the famed Edinburgh Castle on top, clear as day. That gully, she explained, had been the city's original sewer.

Ysolda and I parted on Princes Street, I planning to wander more and she off to her studio to finish getting ready for the festival. I tucked into an ancient graveyard to get my bearings. I saw mid-March crocuses and snowdrops, the beginnings of daffodils, blooming Lenten roses, a low, still-bare tree sporting bright pink panicles of flowers. I saw lush green grass and I smelled moist earth. So different from the frozen Maine I'd just left.

Beyond the wrought-iron gates was a bustling Princes Street, with its chain stores, its Boots pharmacy, Waterstones bookstore, and Marks & Spencer department store. I passed the tall black spires of Arthur's Seat and then a fortress of a hotel beyond which lay a bridge spanning a sea of train tracks leading into Edinburgh Station. Accents drifted in and out, beautiful bubbling snippets, and I couldn't stop smiling.

Just past 9:00 AM and already my lack of sleep was starting to hit. I'd committed to staying awake all day, come hell or high water, both to battle jetlag and to enjoy every second of my four-day stay.

If my plan was to work, I needed more caffeine—which came in the welcome form of a neighborhood coffee spot recommended by Ysolda. Through the tiny door, I stepped into a warm space with white walls and succulents and good music, its hand-lettered signage and table of cakes all signifying the international language of hipster. A sincere and friendly staffer labored to make the perfect foam heart in my drink.

I wandered across the street to the Scottish National Portrait Gallery. (Rather, I scampered across the street while nervously glancing back and forth and back and forth.) They had a special exhibit dedicated to the Great War. It was poignant and heartbreaking. One picture in particular got me. In it, four men were lounging on the grass, cigarettes in fingers, smiling for the camera, their army tents in the background. Their faces were sweet, young, full of both dread and potential. Three of them would be killed in action later that day, a card beneath the picture said. The fourth would be seriously wounded. A sobering reminder of the collective trauma this nation endured barely fifty years ago.

Everyone had told me I needed to visit the Royal Mile, a historic road that begins at the base of the Old Town and runs up, up, up its spine to the castle. After a quick lunch at the museum, I headed there next, crossing the bridge over the rail lines, passing the ornate facade of the Scotsman Hotel, until I reached the street.

A gilded shop sign advertising cashmere jumped out at me. Then another. And another. Each marked charming storefronts with quaint window boxes and inviting window displays. My quickening pulse and grabby hands slowed as I realized that each store carried nearly identical goods, mostly plaid scarves, neatly stacked by color. Some stores also had men's and women's sweaters, a few went so far as to offer kilts. But mostly, just scarves. One particularly sympathetic saleswoman pointed me to the scarves that were actually made in Scotland, whispering that I should always ask.

After a brief stop in the St. Giles' Cathedral, I went back outside to ogle yet more shops advertising cashmere, gorgeous tweeds, and bottle after bottle of whisky. I realized I was in the classier Edinburgh version of San Francisco's Fisherman's Wharf.

Back down to Princes Street I went, this time to marvel at the size of the mystery section at Waterstones and try on an antique ruby ring worth more than my car. My touristing had carried me through most of the day, but it was far from over. I returned to my hotel to check into my room, download more maps and bus schedules, and then I headed off again.

I was staying on the same street as Edinburgh's best Vietnamese restaurant, also known as Edinburgh's *only* Vietnamese restaurant. I stepped in for my requisite jetlag-fighting bowl of pho. Several minutes of blissed slurping later, I left and caught a bus for the city's Old Town. Navigating streets that were already starting to look familiar, I found my way to a pub whose name I'd written down. Inside, knitters awaited.

A Playful Day podcaster Kate Long had traveled up from London and organized the gathering with some twenty or so teachers, designers, vendors, and knitters attending the show. I looked around and spotted knitters in a room to my right, already sprawled around two enormous tables covered with half-empty glasses. Needles were flying.

A smiling man stood up, his bespectacled face familiar to me from photographs. This was Tom van Deijnen, better known to the knitting world as Tom of Holland. Not only is he a master of visible mending, but he also has a superb collection of obscure and intriguing old knitting books. We shook hands and yelled introductions. Women scooted down the bench to make room for me. I sat down, Kate put a gin and tonic in my hand, and I didn't move for the rest of the evening.

Across from me sat the young Finnish designer Veera Välimäki, knitting away on a black sweater. ("She has young eyes," whispered the woman next to me.) To my right, *Curious Handmade* podcaster Helen Stewart told me of her move to the United Kingdom from Australia. Gradually, the pitch of the room grew louder and louder until I couldn't even hear myself. Perhaps another gin and tonic wasn't the wisest idea. I made my exit and hailed a cab for home, making it back to my room just before the clock struck ten. A minute later, I was asleep, forty hours after I'd last seen a bed.

Who ever came up with that myth about beating jetlag by staying up all day? I would like to tell that person that he is cruel and wrong. I awoke feeling worse than the night before. But getting upright and sipping a cup of tea—courtesy of the kettles, mugs, and tea bags so prevalent in UK hotel rooms—worked wonders. Soon I was dressed and out the door for a proper pot of tea and Scottish breakfast complete with plump sausages and thick white toast slathered in marmalade. Belly full and several hours behind schedule but now feeling human, I boarded my bus for the show.

The Edinburgh Corn Exchange was built in 1909 in the Chesser suburb of Edinburgh. Originally designed as a space for farmers and merchants to trade cereal grain, the vast halls of the Corn Exchange had been converted into an event hall that would, for the next two days, host the Edinburgh Yarn Festival.

The show was only in its second year, the first one taking place at a much smaller venue near town and lasting just a single day. That trial run had been a wild success, but still, the move to the Corn Exchange had been a gamble. Would people travel this far out of the city center just for yarn? And would they pay the increased admission price to do so?

The organizers were two passionate and impressively organized knitters named Jo and Mica (pronounced *Meeca*). They managed to bring in nineteen top teachers and program two full days of morning and afternoon workshops. They expanded the marketplace to more than 100 vendors—each handpicked. They booked another hall just for gathering, and they made sure everyone would have constant access to tea, coffee, and cakes. Classes sold out, word spread, and by the time I got to the Corn Exchange on Saturday morning, the place was humming.

"Hello, loves," men in suits greeted us at the door. "Tickets? Straight away you go then. . . ." Nearly all the workshops I'd wanted had been booked for weeks in advance, so I was here strictly for the marketplace.

When I taught at Knit Nation, attendance in my rather geeky yarn and wool classes was sparse. "It's not you," Alice Yu assured me. "They're just not there yet. But it's important that you be here and teach your classes." In the few years that had passed, the future Alice foretold was definitely here. The market was packed with more British knitting yarns than I'd ever seen in one place; people were leaving with armfuls.

Visually, one knitting marketplace can be very much like another. There are only so many ways you can display skeins of yarn. But the character of the vendors and the variety of goods, that is what changes—as well as the spirit of the shoppers.

This marketplace was packed. But I felt no elbows, and saw no greedy grabbing of skeins, no hoarder hustle to beat me to the next booth. All I felt was a calm, focused politeness. I remembered a conversation I'd had with my flight attendant Rick on the way over.

"It's kind of a favorite sociological experiment for me," he'd said. "I can have row after row of passengers who are polite, who make eye contact and say 'please' and 'thank you,' and then I'll reach someone who doesn't even look at me, who barks orders." He leaned in and whispered, "I'll let you guess which one was the American." I smiled politely, realizing he was technically insulting us both, too.

I made a quick pass of two of my favorite natural dyers, feeling virtuous in my restraint, before walking by a coffee stand and running headfirst into Eden Cottage yarns. I let out a moan, and the woman next to me laughed.

In case you aren't familiar with it, there is an international code of yarn marketplace etiquette. The moan, gasp, or uncontrolled giggle is knitterspeak for "I am overwhelmed by what I see and may become unable to restrain myself." When you hear it, you understand that you will not judge but instead will offer support and encouragement—and nothing will be remembered in the morning. I was relieved when the women around me gave the international nod and smile of agreement.

Having fallen off my yarn wagon within just a few minutes of entering the show, the rest came all too quickly. More skeins tumbled into my bag, which turned into another bag, and another.

In the midst of all the color, my eyes found solace in the one booth whose contents were all white. I was impressed by the quality of the fibers and ingenuity of their spinning, including their choice of the trademarked New Merino fiber from Australia, which pledges to be mulesing free. Mulesing is a procedure in which skin is removed, usually without anesthesia, from the tail end of a sheep. The infestation it prevents—flystrike—is even more gruesome and painful. But here we had yarn from farms that had pledged not to do it, experimenting with more humane ways to protect their animals.

Standing next to his yarn was John, a second-generation wool merchant who grew up accompanying his father on wool- and mohair-buying expeditions, even to the once-vast warehouses in San Angelo, Texas. Today, he takes great pride in knowing exactly where to go for the best of any particular kind of fiber, as well as which mills are best equipped to spin each blend properly. He bemoaned the fact that people didn't really seem to care about these details anymore, and it was all I could do to convince him otherwise.

I was in another booth when I overheard the owner tell a customer about the skein she was holding. It was Shetland from the Wadley flock in County Durham, he explained. He'd sent it to Paul at the Halifax Spinning Mill in Yorkshire. I decided to test him on another skein, this one fingering-weight Romney. "Ah!" he said with a smile. "That was a last-minute addition." He went on to tell me how he'd gone to the mill to collect yarn for the show, and Paul told him about 200 fleeces he'd just bought from a local farmer and spun on a whim. Here was a sincere and unpretentious local yarn at its best. It was hard for me to believe that just a few short years before farmers were burning fleeces for lack of customers.

The American-in-Amsterdam designer and knitting personality Stephen West was sharing a booth with Ysolda, and they'd kindly offered to host a signing for me. Stephen gave me a hug and asked what new and exciting things I'd seen. I was embarrassed to admit I'd only managed one aisle so far.

I met sisters who'd traveled all the way from Greece to the show. I met Irene the knitter, and her non-knitting daughter who makes up for not knitting by finding her mother the best brooches and shawl pins. I met

Michelle and saw a picture of her miniature dachshund Bertie Biggles. Among the many Canadians, Australians, and US expats I met, a common theme prevailed: Knitting has helped them slip into what they uniformly described as a difficult-to-penetrate British culture.

Up next was a coffee date with Tom of Holland, with whom I'd only been able to exchange a handful of words at the pub the previous night. A Dutchman now living in Brighton, England, Tom impressed me with his passion for the unsung art of mending and making do.

Perched on stools at a sunny window table, heart-topped espresso drinks between us, we talked. Tom's mind was full of the obscure. He had friends in museums and libraries and universities, and he'd even attended a MEND*RS Symposium—something I didn't know existed until then.

He'd trained as a radiotherapy radiographer (I made him repeat that twice) before getting recruited by a software company to train others on their system. From there, he moved to software testing and was now a team leader. He negotiated a four-day work week so that he would be able to spend three days each week on more fibery pursuits.

We carried our conversation into the supermarket across the street, where we pulled together a picnic supper to enjoy before the evening program began. Ogling the Hobnobs and custards and puddings, we both professed a fondness for grocery shopping in foreign countries. He told me about the store in France that had two long aisles of wine and one small shelf marked "Other Countries." I added a box of his partner's favorite tea to my basket, and a packet of Garibaldi's biscuits, along with a small cake he insisted I try.

It was dark when we returned for the evening program. It had been dubbed the "Ca-BAA-Ret," with entertainment by sound artist, knitwear designer, and author Felicity Ford, plus door prizes and a pub quiz moderated by Felicity and Ysolda. The price of admission also got you one drink ticket, and by the time we arrived people were well into their cups.

At 7:00 PM Felicity—who goes by Felix—strapped a candy apple–red accordion to her chest and launched into a sweetly sung, entertainingly rewritten, knitting-filled version of the show tune "Cabaret."

As the evening wore on and the alcohol took hold, the laughter grew louder and freer. The pub quiz was more challenging than any quiz I'd taken. Working in teams by table, we were given snippets of yarn and asked to match them with possible choices of brand and yarn names—and even the vendors of those yarns were hard-pressed to get it right. We had pages of questions, and then there was a brief break while each group was tasked with making a sheep from the bag of fiber, pipecleaners, and plastic toy eyes on our tables. As the visiting sheep expert, I'd been asked to judge that piece of the quiz, so I got up and wandered the room. Things fell apart when we were asked to list UK locales that had a sheep breed *and* a cheese named after them. After judging was complete (my table didn't win, though we put up a valiant effort), people kept running up to the podium with their iPhones to prove the existence of one small flock—their uncle's or cousin's—where cheese also happened to be made.

I shared a cab with several teachers headed for a hotel downtown, leaping out at my hotel along the way and bidding them goodnight. I checked my phone once more before falling asleep, noticing that Shetland knitting legend Hazel Tindall had just added me on Twitter. A surreal ending to a perfect day.

The next morning was much the same, the bleary beginning, the tea-based revival, the hearty Scottish breakfast. It was Mother's Day in the United Kingdom, and families kept streaming into the restaurant, mothers holding flowers and balloons with "I love you" printed in big cheerful lettering.

Once back at the festival, I made more feeble attempts to conquer the marketplace, and again, I failed. More local yarn fell into my bag, more breed-specific wools. I had a long talk with the manager of a historic wool mill I'd tracked and admired from afar for years. "You'll have to come visit," she'd said. Now I knew I would.

The afternoon found me back in the lounge where the previous night's party had taken place. At the end of the room, a team of T-shirted volunteers was working up a sweat winding skeins of yarn for people and collecting donations for the Teapot Trust, a UK charity that provides art therapy for children with chronic illnesses. (Another team was operating the coat check out front, taking suggested donations per coat.)

But I didn't need any skeins wound. I was too busy gazing at the cakes. Dense carrot and dark, moist chocolate, heaping plates of scones all lined up along the bar. As I waited my turn in line, a woman lifted a fluted cake stand onto the counter. On it, I recognized the telltale chestnut-brown, lumpy form of fruitcake. Not the rum-sodden dreck that has given fruitcake a universally bad reputation, but literally a cake filled with dried fruit, raisins mostly, tasting of that exquisite smoky tang of caramelization. I thought back to the events I've attended in the United States, the convention-center fare, the soggy sandwiches and plastic-bagged Crisco cakes that had come from a cardboard box. What a contrast.

Knitters were sprawled and chatting, fingers stitching away independently of eyes, in an area marked the "podcast lounge," where six popular British podcasters hosted events throughout the weekend. In the rest of the room, people chatted at tables in groups of two or three. The spirit was quiet and calm, with an industrious sense of focus from the ever-swirling swifts and ball winders in the corner.

Sated with cake, I made one final sprint through the marketplace before the 5:00 witching hour struck. Already, most of the vendors had begun dismantling and packing. I made a stop in Tom's classroom, where he was tidying up tables of swatches and snippets and darning mushrooms in colorful shapes and different materials.

"This is my favorite one," he said as he handed me a plain wooden mushroom that was flat on one side. I stared at it.

"Other side," he said. I turned it.

"No, other side." I flipped it upside down. He came over and adjusted my grip.

"Do you see it?" There, in faint pen marks, some previous owner— probably a child being forced to learn darning in school—had drawn the perfect angry grimace.

I walked out with him and we said our goodbyes, standing on opposite sides of the street while he waited for his cab to the airport, I for my bus back to town. We took turns pantomiming outrage and impatience to one another until my bus came. Already, I missed him.

What was different about this event? I asked myself. Was it just its newness, or was there something else? A warmth and inclusiveness to the show that I hadn't experienced back home? Devoid of any corporate overtones or interpersonal melodrama? Or was it just not being among the American cast of characters I knew so well? Maybe, was it simply the glow and romance of travel once again making a liar of me?

Many of the large American shows have taken to encouraging people to buy packages of classes, offering greater discounts the more you take. I'm sure this helps them fill the classes and pay the bills, but it often leads to an empty marketplace during class hours—which hurts vendors. Here, it turned out that most people registered for just one workshop, leaving them loads of time to peruse the marketplace and mingle in the lounge. Vendors were happy, students relaxed and connected.

All weekend, organizer Jo wore a button that said "It'll Be Fine," co-organizer Mica had a necklace with enormous gold letters spelling out "WOOL." While there was never a moment when they didn't seem in total control, this was not *their* event, which is to say it was not, even for a moment, *about* them. They weren't promoting a book or magazine or yarn store or company, they were simply intent on producing an outstanding event. Which they did, in spades.

I was invited to brunch the next morning with Ysolda, Stephen West, and his co-American-in-Amsterdam conspirator Nancy Marchant, the queen of brioche stitch. They were going to Peter's Yard on the university campus, Ysolda said. They'd be lazily knitting and eating cardamom buns. Would I come?

After another bus ride, there was Ysolda and her bike. Nancy had already ordered her coffee. Soon Stephen joined us, resplendent in mint-green spandex leggings with electric pink and blue stripes. For hours we sat, talking, sipping, and knitting. If not for the different currency and accents, and for the fact that it was Scotland outside, we could have been any-where. But more than that, we could have been anywhere *and* we were all completely at home. Nancy helped Ysolda untangle a yarn she'd frogged the night before—"The thing is," Ysolda joked, "I'm really bad with yarn."—while Stephen plugged away at a sweeping sheet of thick, Technicolor brioche fabric.

That morning reinforced something I've long held true, that knitting has a profound connective power. The culture and people and rituals around it, the values, they all contribute to an immediate and profound trust in one another. It's home. You belong and are accepted, which rings true no matter where you are.

I spent the rest of the afternoon racing through Edinburgh much like I'd raced through the marketplace when I knew it was about to close. I chased cashmere and tweed, scones and clotted cream, books, museums, even greenhouses in the Royal Botanic Garden.

Along the way, I picked up an Old Scots word for dreariness: *dreich*. The man who taught it to me sold gorgeous cashmere scarves made in Scotland and had just finished reciting a Robert Burns poem to me. *Dreich*, he explained, "means ... nothingness." He pointed outside and said, "It means *that*," referring to the gray spitty skies that hadn't once shown the sun while I'd been there. *Dreich*. A perfect word both in sound and meaning.

At last I returned to my street for a final bowl of pho, this time in the company of Ysolda. We fantasized that she was going to buy houses all over the world, and that I would move to the United Kingdom. She warned me that the winters were barely better than in Maine.

"People don't realize how far north we are," she said. "It's dark at 8:30 in the morning and it's dark by 3:00 in the afternoon. If you've ever wondered why I get so much done in January, it's because ... there's nothing else to do."

That night I lay in bed trying to fall asleep, my mind going into overdrive processing everything I'd seen on this too-brief trip. I could actually feel myself lending the imprint of past to this experience. I had to open my eyes to remember I was still here, that Edinburgh was still around me. I hadn't left, but already my mind was preparing me for the odd reality of soon being back in Portland, Maine. Would this all feel like a dream?

I thought again about Paul Theroux and his immense dislike for air travel, the sense-numbing way it forces us into a metal tube that's flung at

500 miles per hour until it deposits us into an alien reality. He much prefers the slow train, the old-fashioned crossing. Even then, though, "You never come all the way back," he'd written. But who has time for that now? Maybe that's one reason I love knitting so much, because it lets me enjoy the experience of getting there, of watching the landscape change from cuff to sleeve.

A glorious, ebullient bird song woke me up early, just one bird, but with the longest and most musical of trills. It was impossible to begrudge it. Soon I would be trundling my yarn-stuffed suitcase down the street toward Haymarket, passing under the yellow beams of each streetlight, trying to soak up every last moment of "now" before it became "then." My airport tram passed a commuter train and I felt a pull at my heart, a wish to be on that train instead. I was ready to go, but not to leave.

Boarding the plane for home, I heard a familiar voice welcome me. "Rick!" I exclaimed. "Clara!" We hugged one another like old friends. How was my trip? Rick asked. Did I like Edinburgh? I tried to talk and realized I couldn't come up with words to express what I'd experienced. As I stuttered, he nodded and smiled. "I know. I know. It's something, isn't it?"

While he expertly soothed a screaming baby a few rows back, I fell sound asleep and didn't wake up until somewhere over Albany. Soon the plane was flying parallel to the Hudson River. To our east stood the empty Rhinebeck fairgrounds, still ten months away from holding their next sheep-and-wool festival. Straight ahead, our decidedly unromantic but necessary destination: Newark.

I like to imagine the people in the plane who were looking out the window, seeing this same view for the first time, and finding themselves unable to control their own smiles, their own butterflies. For them, this was new and exciting and oh so glorious. Even the dirty snow, the garbage, the long TSA line after customs, it would all take on a golden hue.

As for me, I would continue my way home to Maine, comforted in the knowledge that I'd added not only to my yarn stash but to my community of friends, and that I'd gotten to witness something very special in its infancy.

ROMANCING THE LOONS:
Holderness, New Hampshire

I AM A CAUTIOUS OPTIMIST by nature. Show me any happy couple and I'll show you potential heartbreak in the making. Having witnessed the dissolution of my parents' marriage, I knew at an early age just how fallible adults could be. All remaining shreds of gullibility had been sent into hiding by my older brothers' merciless teasing. Yet I still knock on wood and read my horoscope and make a wish when I see a shooting star. All of which is to say that when I received my invitation to speak at Squam Art Workshops, a five-day retreat renowned for its *woo-woo* qualities, I was skeptical but also secretly excited.

Prior to launching these creative gatherings in 2008, founder Elizabeth Duvivier was an adjunct professor of English literature, composition, and creative writing at the New Hampshire Institute of Art. But in terms of the knitting world, she came out of nowhere, with a name that seemed to belong in flowery cursive on the cover of a romance novel.

So, too, did Squam come out of nowhere. One day, everybody who was anybody in the knitting world was there, posting pictures of a dock, a lake, twinkle lights, and women in handknits holding hands as they wandered through the woods. They all proclaimed the same thing, that Squam was *magic*.

In 2015, Elizabeth invited me to come give a talk about my work with the American textiles industry at the spring retreat. "Naturally, you don't need to stay the whole weekend," she wrote, "but if you wanted to, you are so welcome!" Having long been curious about the inner machinations of this event, I accepted.

When I told other knitters I was finally going to Squam, they all sighed wistfully and said, "You'll love it." Nobody was able to explain exactly *why* I would love it, they were just incredulous that I hadn't yet been. When pressed for details, they could only add something along the lines of, "It's special. You'll see."

My mother had booked my first therapy session when I was eight. She exposed my brothers and me to *est* and consciousness-raising, self-help gurus and crystals, to such an extent that as an adult, whenever I encounter a group of people who gather in the woods and can't quite explain what happens, only that *it's magic*, all my cult bells go off. Could it be that Squam Lake is breeding ground for more than one kind of loon?

Wary but hopeful, I packed my flip-flops, my mosquito repellant, and my trusty flashlight, and I set out for New Hampshire.

Squam Art Workshops take place at the Rockywold Deephaven Camps, an old-fashioned family vacation resort on Squam Lake. This sublime 6,791-acre freshwater lake straddles three counties in central New Hampshire. It's just a two-hour drive from Portland, but it felt a world away. Roads got narrower and narrower as I went, one landscape more exquisite and bucolic than the next. At last, once my wheels touched dirt, I opened the windows and was hit with a rush of rustling leaves, birds, and, in the distance, the waters of the lake, which sounded like a thousand dogs lapping at their bowls.

It is, without exception, the most exquisite place I've ever been for a knitting retreat. This same lake was immortalized on film in *On Golden Pond*, starring Katharine Hepburn and Henry Fonda. Here you'll find childhood summertime nostalgia perfectly preserved as if pressed within the pages of a diary. The sprawling camps date back to 1897 and 1901, when two neighboring properties (Rockywold and Deephaven) began offering wholesome summer getaways for families. The properties were combined in 1918. Year after year, people returned, families grew, cabins were added. Today, guests can choose from among sixty-two lakeside cabins—each unique and equally charming—and three larger lodges, each with names like Easterleigh and Sheltering Pines.

Rockywold Deephaven Camps operate from May to September. Reservations start each spring in what is really more of an *application* process, with layers of priority and seniority that pretty much guarantee that the same families will be there during high season, year after year, generation after generation. Payment is accepted in the form of cash or check only, and a family of four can easily spend more than $5,000 a week.

It's old school to the core, with a Thursday-night talent show, Friday-night square dance, and a weekly all-camp barbecue on the ball field every Wednesday, weather permitting. Your full American plan includes assigned tables and a dress code in the dining room. "Casual sportswear is acceptable for breakfast and lunch," notes the forty-eight-page guest manual, "but more appropriate dress is recommended for dinner (non-athletic shorts, pants, collared shirt for men; dresses, skirts, pants, non-athletic shorts for women)." As guests of the camp, the dress code applied to us as well.

The spring Squam retreat is the camp's first big shakedown sail of the season, and the fall retreats are the last few easy cruises before they drain the pipes and lock everything up for the winter. Our June retreat had 175 guests, giving us nearly full run of the camp. But once the season is operating at full steam, a staff of 125 serves the needs of 450 guests each week.

I was staying in what Elizabeth called the teacher's cabin, Eldorado, a seven-bedroom cottage just fifty-three feet away from the lake. All the bedrooms but one were shared, everyone thrown together like summer campers on their first trips away from home. Some of my cabinmates were strangers, there to teach classes on drawing and book altering. But most were actually longtime friends and colleagues, including Bristol Ivy, Amy Christoffers, Amy Herzog, Kate Atherley, and Gudrun Johnston. Also in our cabin, but not teaching, were Ysolda Teague and the founders of Ravelry, Jessica and Casey Forbes.

You can't really talk about Squam without talking about Ravelry. To a certain degree, the former wouldn't exist without the help of the latter. As Casey explained to me one night over s'mores, Elizabeth had attended an arts retreat on the West Coast and decided to start up something similar in New Hampshire. She remembered that her old friend Jessica had just started a knitting site called Ravelry. She asked for help, and Jess gave her a list of people she should approach about teaching knitting classes—pretty much the top names in the industry at that time. Ravelry commanded such renown and cred that its unofficial endorsement helped

Elizabeth woo the best. Jess promoted the event on Ravelry, and it filled.

That was just one year after Ravelry's own launch, but the site's galvanizing effect on the knitting community had been swift and profound. We'd already begun the migration from a small, tightly controlled analog universe to a democratized digital one. But here, in Ravelry, we had a one-stop shop for knitters to connect, to learn and share, to find out about yarns and patterns. Readers eagerly populated the site with content, and designers found themselves able, at last, to sell their patterns directly to the public.

Such sophisticated technology would have been impossible for any fledgling knitting player to afford, but this one had a secret weapon. Founder Jessica Forbes, who had only learned to knit in 2004 from the books *Stitch 'n Bitch* and *Knitting For Dummies*, was married to Casey, a brilliant technologist with state-of-the-art Ruby on Rails programming skills. They launched Ravelry together, and theirs was a killer combo. Ravelry didn't just disrupt the industry, it created a whole new one that has become what many people now think of when they hear the word *knitting*. By the time we arrived at Squam, Ravelry had just topped 5.3 million registered users.

We all gathered on Wednesday night after dinner in an old building that overlooks a pair of well-preserved tennis courts. Knitted flowers twisted along the backs of benches and up the porch railings. Colorful bunting and twinkle lights, pompoms and a roaring fire transformed the playhouse into a magical space. We sat, happy, eager, apprehensive. The smell of wood smoke mingled with mosquito repellant. A woman in a linen wrap dress with long, flowing hair ascended the stage and spread her arms out to welcome us—Elizabeth.

"I . . . I just need to ground a moment," she said somewhat breathlessly, waving her hands and closing her eyes. We smiled and waited. "Let's close our eyes and breathe," she said in a singsong voice. "Breathing in . . . out . . . in . . . out . . ." I listened to our collective exhales, measuring my sprinting distance to the door.

Elizabeth came to life. Excited, she wanted to tell us how much she had changed since she launched Squam in 2008, and how even the *event* was a completely transformed experience. In fact, she hadn't played any part in planning this year's retreat. It was all the work of others, who we cheered and applauded when she asked them to stand. Another exciting transformation was that she would be teaching a workshop on writing this year (more applause).

It was all, she said, because of a chance encounter she'd had the previous fall, the night before her fall retreat was to begin. She had gathered with some friends. She'd left her cabin to find a suitable spot to work some moon magic for the group when a loud hiss came from the cabin porch: "Skunk!" (We all gasped.)

Sure enough, standing on the path between her and the cabin was a great big skunk. Elizabeth was filled with terror. Tomorrow, she thought, 170 people would arrive, each expecting a hug from her. How can you run an event when reeking of skunk?

Heart racing, she slowly inched toward the lake—only to have the skunk follow her. (More gasps.)

Elizabeth was a skillful storyteller. She deftly led our collective anticipation ever closer to the brink of disaster. Only then, at last, did she tell us how she opened her eyes and saw that the skunk had walked away. The minute she knew she was safe, Elizabeth told us how she felt a powerful rush of confidence come over her, a rush of pure fearlessness.

She had looked up the symbolism of the skunk, wondering what kind of message the universe may have been trying to send her. "The skunk," she explained, "is a symbol of protection, independence, and self-respect." She held up a small figurine of a skunk that she has carried with her ever since. We cheered again.

One by one, she invited the teachers up to introduce themselves and to break the ice by answering a question: What are your favorite shoes? We heard talk of Converse sneakers, of Dr. Martens and Frye boots, of original wood-bottomed Dr. Scholl's, and of preferring to go barefoot.

In closing, Elizabeth urged us to own the fullness of who we are, to use kindling only for starting fires, and, on Saturday night, to carpool to the marketplace because parking would be tight.

"There are gifts waiting for you in these woods," she told us, "and I hope that you find them." I knew that the woods offered ticks and mosquitoes and apparently skunks, but I don't think those were the gifts she meant. The woods also offered bears, like the one that tried to break into the teacher's cabin a few years ago.

"Bears I didn't get to see," Ysolda complained on the walk back to our cabin, "because Franklin [Habit] has the completely wrong priorities." His priority had been to scare the bear away rather than wake up Ysolda so she could Instagram it. "For the record," she added, "if you see a bear and I am in the building, I would like to be alerted."

We stumbled through darkness, our path lit by small flickering pools of light from LED headlamps, cell phones, and the little Duracell flashlight I've had by my bed since college. Once safely inside, door closed against marauding nature, Ysolda set about making us all hot toddies while someone else built us a roaring fire.

The cabins are perfectly preserved examples of what a wealthy Bostonian rusticator would have wanted at the turn of the last century. Which is to say, they have no phones or TVs, no stoves, coffee makers, hair dryers, or microwaves. Wi-Fi access has been reluctantly added, but it's spotty. The only heat comes from your fireplace, which is stocked with perfectly cut, split, and seasoned firewood supplied every morning by a brigade of handsome young men. Beds all have thick comforters to keep you warm—and it will be just you alone in bed, because every bed on the property is a twin. (I guess those rusticators didn't believe in hanky-panky, either.)

Like bank robbers on the run, we had stocked our cabin with enough food for a month-long standoff. We had potato, corn, and kale chips, as well as olives, cheeses, salamis, sesame snacks, crackers, coconut water, every kind of coffee and tea, and of course, a full supply of graham crackers, marshmallows, and chocolate bars for s'mores. Jess and Casey had even thought to bring sticks for roasting the marshmallows over our fire.

While cabins have no refrigerators, they do have their original iceboxes. Preserving the spirit of authenticity, they don't just truck in the ice, they actually cut it from the lake each January and store it in sawdust-filled ice houses. Yet more handsome young men come to the cabins each morning with freshly painted green wheelbarrows of ice, inspecting and replenishing each icebox as necessary.

Our icebox was full of booze, every kind of beer, wine, and cider. Sharing the cabin was teacher and designer Thea Colman, better known under her moniker BabyCocktails. ("If you Google 'Thea Colman' you'll get a porn star," she said when we met.) In keeping with her nickname, she had brought a big bottle of gin, a bag of limes, and plenty of tonic.

I would be bunking with Bristol Ivy, who had recently fledged from Brooklyn Tweed and was striking out on her own as a designer—and who also happens to live one block away from me in Portland. Ysolda was bunking with Gudrun downstairs, closest to the door through which any bear might try to pass. Jess and Casey had brought their baby, August, who goes by the name Auggie and whose face is so sincere and expressive that it would melt even the most hardened of hearts. Jess had brought foam earplugs for everyone just in case he started screaming in the night, but he ended up being the quietest among us. Their older daughter, Eloise, was enjoying time alone with her grandma back home.

We assembled early the next morning, spraying ourselves with an array of bug sprays according to our personal philosophies about chemicals and itching, and walked through the woods to get to breakfast. In the morning light, I could see that the paths had been dotted with yet more pompoms, a tiny knitted flower here, a garland there.

Meals were served in a huge old dining hall, with a cold buffet of fruits and yogurts and a hot buffet fully stocked with eggs, sausages, bacon, pancakes, and the like.

"The *real* maple syrup is over here!" Jess grabbed my elbow and steered me over to a table with a big pump-topped jug of New Hampshire's finest. "Can you believe it?" We quickly discovered that we shared similar snack cravings, and whenever Jess reached for a bag or box, she brought it over for me to try.

The camp is spread across 200 acres, and many people preferred to drive to meals, which caused a bit of a traffic jam outside. At breakfast, and every meal thereafter, announcements would be made about which car was improperly parked. "A Subaru Forester is blocking the offices," we'd be told, prompting all twenty-one people owning Subaru Foresters to get up and head for the door simultaneously.

In 1930, the camp began keeping track of who'd caught the biggest fish of the season. The names hung on a plaque over the coffee station, older ones written in perfect gold lettering, newer ones in sloppy pen. Arthur Howe took the lead that first year, for nabbing a four-and-a-half-pound, nineteen-inch bass. He was unseated the following year by N. S. Davis, who was knocked off the pedestal in 1932 by none other than a *Mrs.* N. S. Davis. After what I imagine to be a very long winter, he finally seized the lead back from his wife in 1933. The fish continued to be caught, even during the war years. I wondered what the story was with Thomas B. McAdams, who took the trophy, in 1948, "for trying."

Most people were taking two six-hour workshops that week, but I'd signed up for just one: an embroidery class taught by artist Joetta Maue. The class was called "Thread and Memory," and it incorporated elements of visual storytelling. Ysolda and I showed up just as the class was beginning in a nearby cabin, a fire already roaring in the fireplace. Joetta was young, with a long floral skirt and hair in a loose bun. Her thick-rimmed glasses kept slipping down her tiny nose, and she rolled her *R*s around on her tongue when she spoke.

We began with another guided meditation. This one was for five minutes, intended to settle us in a grounded, creative place. *Fine,* I told myself, *I'll do your meditation, but so help me god, I'm not coming back after lunch.* But as it turned out, there may have been something to those guided meditations. Not only did I come back after lunch, but I found myself unable to put down my embroidery for the rest of the day.

You do a lot of walking at Squam. As you walk, you find yourself staring into the windows of each cabin you pass, wondering what it must be like inside. Elizabeth took notice, because this year she added a Thursday-night Cabin Crawl. We'd all been given a small painting. Those who wanted to open their cabins to visitors simply needed to hang the painting on their door. You could walk from cabin to cabin, peek inside, meet people. The only question became who stayed in the cabin to welcome visitors and who got to tour the others. I wouldn't know how this played out because our cabin was at the end of a long path and we decided to keep our door shut for the night.

While I toiled away at my tidy little embroidery project, Ysolda, always one to go big, had opted to embroider the entire map of the Squam property over a bedspread-sized piece of gossamer fabric. Meanwhile, Jess had taken a rug-hooking class that day and was sitting next to me, her rug-hooking frame awkwardly perched on her lap.

"There were a lotta hooker jokes today," she sighed. "A *lotta* hooker jokes." After a pause, and another sigh, she added, "I don't think I'm going to be taking up rug hooking any time soon." She reached for a jar and handed it to me. "Olive?"

Meanwhile Casey played DJ over a small Bluetooth-powered speaker, with regular input from Ysolda and Bristol, the resident young'uns of the cabin (both under thirty).

On Friday, while everyone else began their second class, I had the day free. Ysolda did too, so we spent most of our time together. Gudrun was teaching her short-rows class in our living room. Thus booted from the cabin, we took our coffee and our knitting out onto the dock.

As we spoke, I looked out onto the placid waters of the lake and noticed a tiny disturbance. A beautiful dragonfly had somehow flopped onto its back and was trapped on the water. Ysolda was talking about the historic significance of women's baseball leagues during World War II, but all I could think was that a dragonfly was drowning, and I couldn't just sit there and watch it die. I love dragonflies.

We had two kayaks tied to the dock, rented by Thea aka BabyCocktails as a gift to the cabin. I undid a knot on the first kayak and slipped off my shoes.

"What are you doing?" Ysolda asked, and I explained.

"I think it's dead," she said, looking over her shoulder.

No it isn't, I thought. I would paddle to the dragonfly and save it.

"I really think it's dead," Ysolda said again.

I lowered myself to my knees and stepped into the kayak, first one foot, then another, but I forgot how narrow kayaks are, and I hadn't quite adjusted my weight accordingly, and when I reached out to my left to regain my balance, I reached too far and, with a big splash, found myself in the water.

"It's dead," Ysolda repeated.

My splash had pushed the now clearly dead dragonfly well beyond reach. And now I had a new problem: I was fully clothed in the lake. My cabin was just fifty-three feet away, but it was filled with students, all sitting in a living room through which I'd have to walk if I wanted to get dry clothes. By the grace of whoever had designed the cabin, they hadn't seen what I'd done.

Ysolda suggested I just strip and let my clothes dry on the dock, as if being naked on the dock in front of a cabin full of students was somehow better than being wet but fully clothed. We decided on a plan B: She would go into the cabin and get towels.

I had been wearing a sweater that was to be the center of my talk in just a few hours. A sweater that was now sopping wet. I carefully took it off and handed it up to Ysolda, who began blotting it with towels. Then I pulled myself out of the lake and onto the dock, something impossible to do with any degree of elegance whether in a bathing suit or, in my case, fully clothed. I wondered if this was what Elizabeth had in mind when she urged us to own the fullness of who we are?

For the next few hours, I sat on the dock with Ysolda, wrapped in a towel, trying not to shiver, feeling quite embarrassed and pretending I wasn't, until I looked dry enough to be able to walk past everyone in the living room without it being obvious that I'd just dunked myself in the lake.

"Hey, maybe the dragonfly is your spirit animal," Jess suggested later that night over chips and salsa. "You should look it up and see what it means!" Remembering Elizabeth's skunk story, I thought what the heck and pulled out my phone. Was this my skunk moment? Would my life be forever changed?

"The dragonfly," I read, "is a creature of the wind. It portends change." The words gave me goose bumps. I read on, "The dragonfly carries messages that relate to our deeper thoughts. It holds the wisdom of transformation and adaptability in life." *Hmmm.*

Half the power of Squam, at *least* half, has to be place. Its remoteness and innocent beauty invite a return to one's childhood, whether real or imagined. You couldn't get that from a Radisson by the airport. People are the other half. Their collective sincerity, enthusiasm, and eagerness to surrender and go deep creates an environment for introspection. We come with the perspective (and the wounds) of adults. But here, in this place, we're given an opportunity to reassess, reexamine, to grapple with ghosts, and quite possibly emerge a slightly more healed person. There's a lot of sitting on docks staring out at the lake, walking through woods, and then sitting in chairs staring into a fire. Even surrounded by people, you have a lot of time to think.

The sound of lapping water becomes a presence. You get used to glimpsing the sparkle of the lake through the leaves. It beckons, and inevitably, you need to go in. On Saturday afternoon, the day after I'd given my talk, Ysolda and I kayaked to lunch. We returned to our cabin's dock, where people were knitting. Several others had donned their bathing suits and swum out to a float. While I paddled around aimlessly in my kayak, Ysolda ran up to the cabin, changed into her bathing suit, and did a perfect dive off the dock.

As my brain was processing what she'd just done, she came up far too soon. She stood upright, holding her face. Her back was toward the people on the dock, but from my kayak, I could already see the blood streaming down her hands. The fact that she was standing at all, waist high, where she'd just dove, should have been our clue. She'd hit a very big boulder.

I guided her back to the dock, where first aid kits were brought out, then packs of ice. Having determined that she didn't need stitches, we propped her in a chair with her knitting. She strapped the ice pack to her head, like a pirate. Certainly *this* wasn't the fullness Elizabeth had urged us to find in ourselves? Ysolda laughed, I presumed, from both shock and embarrassment. But the vision of her dive would haunt me. I know each of us silently echoed thoughts of just how very bad it could have been, and how lucky we were that she was okay.

That night was the Squam Art Fair, a massive marketplace that brings vendors and even more customers from as far away as Canada. More bunting and twinkle lights were hung, and freshly carved ice lanterns illuminated pathways to the market building. Part of my arrangement with Elizabeth was that I got a spot in the marketplace to sell skeins of my Clara Yarn and help recoup my transportation costs. But when I went inside and asked where I should set up, they gave me a funny look. Didn't I know? I wasn't in here. I was in the small cottage across the road, where the Ravelry VIP lounge would be set up. Only I knew from talking with Jess and Casey that they weren't planning on being there this year because of the baby. So basically, I would be all alone with a keg of beer in a cabin across the road from everyone else. It was impossible not to feel lousy, to take this expulsion personally.

Amy Herzog helped me absorb the new reality of my situation, advising which yarns should go where, stacking precious skeins of painstakingly sourced Cormo and Shetland wool, until my little table area—aided by props Bristol brought down from Portland—looked, dare I suggest, rather magical.

I tried not to glance across the street at where the *real* action was, at all the vans and cars and trucks streaming in, vendors unloading and setting up. I closed the door of my silent cabin, walked to dinner, and gave myself a pep talk. "You are *not* going to indulge in self pity," I told myself. "Do. Not. Cry."

Mid-macaroni and cheese, my phone buzzed. It was designer Hannah Fettig, who'd come down with her husband, Abe, for the night. "They're lining up!" she said. "Better get down there!"

As I got closer, I saw not one line but two: One leading to the main marketplace, the other straight to my little cabin. Amy directed me around to a back entrance. I slipped in, readied myself, and opened the door.

What followed was the knitterly version of *It's a Wonderful Life*. One by one, they came. And they kept coming, smiling, eager, friendly, open, arms laden with my yarn, for three solid hours. Instead of sitting alone and pretending it didn't matter, pretending I wasn't humiliated or that this didn't symbolize every doubt I had about my career up to that point, I was swamped.

My cabinmates never left my side. Each kept offering water, restocking help, beer, even just a smile to boost my energy. At some point in the night, vendors had jammed the Wi-Fi signal across the road and couldn't process credit cards at all. "Are you able to get online?" Casey whispered over my shoulder after I finished with one person, "Because I can get you online if you need. Just let me know." Here was the grand wizard of Ravelry, offering me his secret backdoor access to the Internet. And better yet, I didn't need it.

Casey and Ysolda, whose face was now swollen and bloodied as if she'd not only seen that bear but gotten into a fist fight with it, were deftly operating the keg while I sold almost every skein I had brought to a line that never slowed. Ysolda had wisely pinned three Ravelry buttons to her sweater. On them she'd written: "I'm OK! (Really)," "I dove off the dock," and "Yes, that was stupid."

I'd made a joke to Casey earlier that day, while on the dock with him and Auggie, a joke about his rapidly expanding empire. It's something we all secretly think about, the powerful behemoth that Ravelry has become.

"I hope not," was Casey's reply. When I asked what he meant, he explained, "Ravelry already supports four families. Shouldn't that be enough?"

He popped a pea puff in Auggie's outstretched hand and added, in a quiet, sincere voice, "I just hope people keep knitting."

The dragonfly wasn't lying. I'd known for some time about the change it was foretelling, the transformation and adaptability it signaled. The industry has undergone a sea change since I started reviewing yarn in 2000. As for my own interests, they, too, have changed. I've wanted to work more on reviving our domestic textiles infrastructure, telling its stories, supporting its few remaining players, in ways I couldn't as a critic. In addition to being a storyteller of other makers, I wanted to become a maker myself. It's been a slow, cautious shift, but each step has opened my heart to people in surprising new ways. My time at Squam, the validation of its community and even the message from that poor little dragonfly, really did help me glimpse the fullness of who I might continue to be.

That night we stumbled back to our cabin, to a roaring fire and yet more s'mores, and to the last of Ysolda's hot toddies. We got in our pajamas and brought our blankets closer to the fire. There we curled up, telling stories, nobody quite willing to acknowledge that it would all end in the morning. Then, after we were all tucked in bed, Bristol and I whispering to each other in the dark, the loons began a hauntingly exquisite series of wails and tremolos that lasted for minutes and left us speechless.

There was no closing ceremony on Sunday, no formal parting, no collective goodbye. Just a series of hugs that went on and on, from dining hall to dock to cabin, until the last suitcase had been shut, the last kale chip eaten. Five days is brief in the grand scheme of things, but it was enough to boost our creative spirits. We were baptized by the lake, serenaded by loons, bitten by bugs, and even bashed by boulders. In need of some quiet and a nap, I packed my car and drove home, back into a slightly more beautiful world. Maybe there was some magic in those woods after all.

ACKNOWLEDGMENTS

I love a good story. The ones Melanie Falick told in *Knitting in America* inspired me to start writing *Knitter's Review*. As we became friends, she encouraged me to venture beyond crimp and ply, trusting me and pushing me ever forward. I'm honored to work with her.

While I've never had the pleasure of meeting Paul Theroux, his sublime travel narratives have kept me eyeing the horizon and always striving for that better sentence. I thought of him often as I wrote this book, wondering what he would make of our knitting world.

I'm grateful to my parents for never wavering in their encouragement—or if they have, they're really good at hiding it. My father faithfully wears his handknitted cashmere scarf; my mother displays my books and collects my yarn even though she doesn't knit a stitch. My brothers and their families have graciously allowed knitting to intrude upon their own lives, too, over-taking conversations and, occasionally, impinging upon vacations. And my heart, Clare, has become the most knitting-aware non-knitter I know, always inspiring me to be a better version of myself. To them—as well as my friend and agent Elizabeth Kaplan—I humbly give thanks.

Nothing exists in a vacuum. My largest debt of gratitude goes to the generations of knitters who came before me, who set the stage for our current culture to flourish, and to the readers of *Knitter's Review*, who, for fifteen years, allowed me to experience the world of yarn in my way. I had no intention of becoming a knitting journalist when I started on this path. I had no clever business plan, no ten-year strategy to cash in. I was simply following my heart. Which, as it turns out, is the best way to do it.